The Life & Times of "Little Johnny Corboy"

VOLUME II

School Daze

John Medford Corboy, MD
with Stephen Dillon, Editor

Editor-in-Chief: Stephen Dillon

Amanuenses: Sharri Verlaine Mendoza
Deira Zayas
Litea Maiava
Sandra Brooke

Cover design by Debra Castro
Design and Layout: Nelson Gaspar
David Walker

Published by: John M. Corboy
Assistant: Jenn Martin
ISBN: 979-8-9897544-0-3
Printed by: Kindle Direct Publishing
Additional Copies: Amazon.com

Newspaper clippings courtesy of
Honolulu Star-Advertiser Archives

www.lifeandtimesoflittlejohnnycorboy.com

Also by John M. Corboy:
Life and Times of "Little Johnny Corboy"
Volume One: "Providence in the Pacific"
Copyright © John M. Corboy 2023
Published by Amazon KDP

The Retinoscopy Book: An Introductory Manual for Eye Care Professionals, Fifth Edition
Copyright © Slack Inc, 2003

60@60: Things that happen to your body, and what you can do about them, With Sally Kurtzman
Copyright © 60@60, LLC, 2008
Published by A Simpler Life Press

WHAT OTHERS HAVE TO SAY ABOUT
LITTLE JOHNNY CORBOY'S VOLUME TWO: SCHOOL DAZE

Here's the intimate story of the medical education of Dr. John Corboy who grew up in Hawaii to become an internationally respected eye surgeon, founder of the Hawaiian Eye Center with nine offices serving all the Hawaiian Islands. He was the humanitarian who led his Hawaiian Eye Foundation to 40 years of charity eye care across the South Pacific, Asian training programs, and hundreds of worldwide volunteer missions.

Surgeon, teacher, broadcaster, humanitarian, and now author. Here's the fascinating story of his education, marriage, and military service. Volume three should be even more fun.

Bob Sigall
Author and Columnist, *Honolulu Star-Advertiser*

Beautiful and nostalgic…so well done! Like JC's first book, this is another delightful autobiography. So many personal and historical photos…married with great stories and life lessons…combining to transport the reader to the 1950s and '60s in the Midwest. All from the lens of a young John Corboy, cramming to become Dr. John, founder of the Hawaiian Eye Center and Foundation. Now I'm looking forward to the third volume in the series!

Dave Blinn
Businessman

John Corboy has been a friend and mentor for almost 40 years and has served as an example of a life well lived. In this book we learn how he crammed four years of pre-medical science into two years, studied medicine at the University of Illinois, served an internship, married his favorite nurse, and was drafted to serve the Coast Guard and Mexican Border Quarantine. John has spliced several lives into one: entrepreneur, sailor, family man, pilot, naturist, smiling curmudgeon, and energizer. Here's the colorful story of his medical education.

John Pinto
International Ophthalmic Practice Management Consultant

I love Corboy's story-telling! This book tells how a mischievous high schooler became a doctor. He really buckled down in college to become a study-maniac; not a single date, but it seems like he made up for that celibacy in medical school! I never realized how heavy pre-med and medical training is! And I enjoyed all those motorcycle stories!

Keith Frost
Automotive Instructor

Here's the second volume in the story of how "Little Johnny Corboy" became the prominent eye surgeon. He studiously knocked-off pre-med in record time, then delighted in his training to become a physician. After his internship and marriage, he's drafted into the US Public Health Service to serve the Coast Guard and border quarantine.

Fascinating historical references for his great-grandchildren. I wish I could have been an exchange student like he was in Germany. I want volume three!

Bill Hewak, M.D.
Vice President Eye Mission of the Pacific

I enjoyed the intimate details of Corboy's college-nerd story and med-school training. That Cat Dissector story really moved me! It shows how a single, almost forgotten event, can completely change one's career - and even life! We seldom know the results of the ripples we create in our daily lives.

I like the references to the role of (Divine) Providence. But those rats and worms, ugh!

Heidi J. Canon
Social Work Consultant

WHAT OTHERS HAVE TO SAY ABOUT

LITTLE JOHNNY CORBOY'S VOLUME ONE: PROVIDENCE IN THE PACIFIC

The book was gifted to me about three weeks ago. From the first 3 minutes of reading it, I was hooked and couldn't put it down. As fan of the U.S. 30's 40's and 50's I couldn't help but love it. Dr. Corboy gives readers a real world view of what things were like yesteryear. With much of story based in Hawaii he also provides a very interesting view of life in paradise during and following WWII. it's a great American story about an American family that might be unknown to many had not this retired accomplished surgeon become an accomplished author."

Ric Tiplady
Ophthalmic Manufacturer's Representative

Dr. John Corboy's book has fascinating stories about growing up in Hawai'i. His tales about school, girlfriends, "boat days," and being a radio station DJ are fun and delightful. Before I knew it, I had read two hundred pages. I'm looking forward to Volume II, to find out what happens next!

Bob Sigall
Columnist, *Honolulu Star-Advertiser*

Dr. Corboy's initial memoir relates his first eighteen years in a brisk and breezy style that's both joyously entertaining and endearing in its honesty. Whether he's "getting switched" or tentatively discovering sexuality, the good doctor scrutinizes it all cheerily and unsparingly. Both charmingly sentimental and humorously self-deprecating, the work features a folksy historical focus, and unique and intimate memories of the still-exotic Hawai'i of the 'Forties and 'Fifties.

Stephen Dillon
Journalist and Sequestration Consultant

As a former kama'āina, reading Life and Times of "Little Johnny Corboy" was an interesting look at postwar Hawai'i as I lived it many years ago. While this was from a young man's point of view, a coming of age in Paradise, it showed Honolulu in particular on a rise from a sleepy city and island ultimately to statehood. I enjoyed all his hijinks and highlights as he matured—just like the islands' growth at that time. I think kama'āina *(old timers) and* malihini *(newcomers) alike will enjoy this romp through childhood to maturity, all aloha style. Well written and detailed with examples and anecdotes, Little Johnny Corboy will be a fun trip to paradise from your couch.*

Sally Kurtzman
Educator

The writings of Dr. John Corboy invoke a feeling similar to the reading of ancient Greek tales—those of rituals, heroes, gods—but in a Hawai'i setting. Corboy's tales include the raw temptations of youth that ran counter to a Catholic upbringing; the brawny heroes of the Sunday evening wrestling matches; a father who could wrest swordfish using only a thread of light tackle. Numerous photographs and historical comparisons throughout the text bring to life the images and memories of John's days gone by—sadly gone, but never forgotten. Wonderful tales these are, and each begs more than one reading.

Bill Hewak
Vice President, Eye Mission of the Pacific

Dedicated to my long-suffering parents, my father Dr. Philip M. Corboy and my mother Clarice Matthewson Corboy, who rolled their eyes and patiently put up with their exasperating, rambunctious boy, and who were ultimately pleased by his accomplishments.

Thanks, Mom and Dad, for your patience, example of good character, work ethic, love, and unfailing support! I couldn't have done it without you.

Love, "Little Johnny"

CONTENTS

CONTENTS

CONTENTS

CONTENTS

CONTENTS

CONTENTS

Preface

BOOK TWO

In *Volume One* of my series, I lamented that my grandfather Stephen hadn't chronicled his life as a college professor at the turn of the Twentieth Century, and particularly his impressions of the first appearance of automobiles and airplanes in his small town of Valparaiso, Indiana.

My thoughtful sister Sally advised, "Stop grumbling about what your grandfather didn't do. You're a grandfather now, so why don't *you* leave a record for your grandchildren and great-grandchildren? Tell them what life was like in your era."

Thus inspired, I sought to bundle my life between two covers, but found that after three hundred pages I had barely done justice to my first eighteen years. I've often said, "Anything worth doing is worth *over*doing," so I soon found myself planning a few more volumes to satisfactorily complete my story.

This book, "School Daze," (1958 – '66) includes my education during college, med school, hospital internship, as well as and my military service in the Coast Guard and Border Quarantine Service during the Viet Nam War era.

In *Part One, College*, you will see the revision of my career plans from broadcasting and communications to medicine, and my transformation into a ferociously obsessed student, in my quest to save an extra year's college expenses. Despite cautions from advisors and doubts from my peers, I completed the three to four year science curriculum in two frenzied and successful years.

In *Part Two, Med School*, there's probably too much detail about how medicine was taught in the '60s, but the information will prove useful for those interested. Today, there is much more emphasis on imaging and Genomics than physical diagnosis (examining the patient); this shift is in many ways lamentable.

In *Part Three, Internship*, I met and courted my bride Mary Jo, and we were married at the conclusion, when I was drafted into military service.

Part Four, Public Health Service, covers my two delightful years medically serving with the Coast Guard in San Diego and the Border Quarantine Station at San Ysidro, California, which led to my choice of specialty — rather than general practice.

I hope you enjoy this story of my decade of early education and training, and the amazing role of *Providence* in my life.

I've already discovered that my grandchildren are unfamiliar with payphones, typewriters, and film-cameras, so I'm adding historical perspectives to my narrative.

Upcoming plans are for *Volume Three* (1966–'75) to detail my additional four years of Ophthalmology Residency training, my initial specialty practice, and the joyous raising of three magnificent children with my beloved Mary Jo.

Volume Four (1975–98) will detail my creation of the *Hawaiian Eye Center* and the groundbreaking medical innovations we developed.

Volume Five (1999–2020) God willing, will cover my 20 "retirement years" managing my *Hawaiian Eye Foundation*, doing hundreds of world-wide charity medical missions and Asian training programs around the world.

So, here's my education story: the first steps in the emergence of a compassionate, empathetic physician-surgeon, from the mischievous, hot-rodding, high school broadcaster of Volume One.

I am deeply indebted to my new team: office manager Nicole Barretto, Chief Editor Steve Dillon, Layout/Design guys Nelson Gaspar and David Walker, and "seeing eyes", my remarkably skillful and patient amanuenses, Sharri Verlaine Mendoza, Litea Maiava and Sandra Brooke. And, as always, my amazing creative "cover girl" Debra Castro. Special thanks to my darling bride Regan, who gives me the time and space for this indulgence.

Mahalo nui.

Little Johnny, 2024

Here's the origin of the series title:

VALPO REMINDER, FRIDAY, OCTOBER 6, 1939

Little Johnny . . .

Little Johnny Corboy one year old
Learned to say "dog-gone" 'thout bein' told,
Turns on the radio and hulas like mad,
Ain't that a dandy start for a little lad?

By Burk

This clipping appeared as a surprise to my parents in the **Valpo Reminder** ***October 6, 1939***

Prologue

In **Volume One** of this series, ***Providence in the Pacific***, I described my youthful magnificent experience at YMCA Camp Harold R. Erdman, when I was ten and twelve years old. We boys learned resilience and self-reliance; we were rewarded by feelings of independence and self-confidence.

Unfortunately, the Camp was not available to my boys growing up, and I recently lamented this to the YMCA. I learned that things were now very different: that Camp was open to extensive programs as explained here by the Executive Director:

> "As Camp Erdman comes up on the celebration of its 100-year anniversary, it continues to serve young people from the islands, and around the world. Camp serves youth, family, and community through programs focused on character and social development, cultural awareness, environmental stewardship, and exposure to new skills and experiences. Since John's time at Camp, hundreds of thousands of young people, families, and community members have created lasting memories and have had transformational experiences here at YMCA Camp Erdman.
>
> Camp is now available for all, regardless of gender, age, background, or faith. Camp provides the opportunity to be surrounded by, and immersed in, aloha ʻāina, sharing in the importance of this place, and the cultural values it embodies. Staff and participants from around the islands and the world gather to learn and appreciate this amazing opportunity!
>
> We look forward with excitement to our next 100 years of youth development and service."

Andrew 'Mish' Hood
Executive Director, YMCA Camp Erdman
69-385 Farrington Hwy., Waialua, HI 96791
www.camperdman.org

Part 1

COLLEGE DAZE

Early photo sent home to my parents.

I

Off to College

September '56: College Dorm

After Uncle Steve dropped me off that Sunday morning, I climbed the steep, imposing stairs to the lobby of the three-story Loyola Hall Men's Dormitory. It felt like a grand adventure living in Chicago, thousands of miles from home, not knowing how difficult college might be, or what my new life would be like. But I had been pretty successful so far, and was confident that I could deal with whatever challenges arose. Because of my scholarship, I knew I'd have to perform very well academically, so "good grades" were my chief concern at the time.

At the front desk I was handed a key to room 321 and headed upstairs. This was a bright, two bed, two desk room with a large window overlooking the back alley below. My roommate had not yet arrived, so I chose half of the closet and the desk near the window and began unpacking. I went down the hall to check out the nearby community bathroom, which contained several showers, basins, and toilets.

Roommate

I finished unpacking; later that afternoon, my roommate, Larry Kaufman, arrived. He lived in a nearby suburb and was pleasant and easy-going, so after he moved in we walked across North Sheridan Road to a family-style restaurant, Cindy Sue's Pizzeria. Pizza was quite a novelty at the time.

After dinner we returned to our room, and spent a couple hours getting acquainted, talking about our families and hobbies, our interests, and our anticipations about our first year in college. Not much about goals and dreams, probably because neither of us *had* any at the time. Like me, Larry was taking a basic liberal arts *Humanities* curriculum, so we shared course lists in History, English Comp, foreign language, Speech, Psychology, and the Catholic school requisite, Theology.

Larry got up early the following morning and headed off for registration. I found the cafeteria, had breakfast, and followed guys walking toward campus. The Loyola

University North Shore Campus was lovely: Ivy-covered old buildings named for benefactors, as well as beautiful trees, and the picturesque Lake Michigan shoreline.

Beanies

I followed the crowd to the Student Union building where we incoming freshmen were processed. We received our student ID cards and freshman beanies, which we were required to wear whenever we were on campus, or risk demerits. I guess this rather demeaning item was meant to humble those among us who may have felt like "big deal college men."

Registration

Registration for classes also took place here in the Student Union. There were tables covered with boxes of IBM punch cards (the first successful attempt at computerized data-collection). We were each given a list of our classes and passed single file along tables with the IBM punch card boxes. There might be, for example, five boxes marked *English Comp 101* and the name of the instructor. Each card box contained as many cards as students were permitted for that particular class. Fifty cards in the box would admit fifty students, and when they were gone, that class was closed, so we'd need to pick from another box. I noticed that some of the boxes were already empty, which indicated the course of a particularly popular teacher. I had no idea which teachers were to be preferred, so I simply picked my cards from boxes marked English Comp 101, Psychology 101, Theology 101, Speech and Rhetoric 101, German 1, and History 101 (Europe to 1500).

At the end of the line my cards were inspected and approved. I was given a class schedule, which began the following morning, along with a book list for each of my courses. Building and room assignments were shown on the class schedule. After I left, I wandered the campus, locating the different buildings I'd be in tomorrow, the beautiful campus church, *Madonna Della Strada* ("MDS", *Our Lady of the Way*), with marvelous stained-glass windows, the administration building, etc. There was also a note stating that I was to report to the bursar as soon as possible to settle my delinquent tuition bill. Since I had the time, I stopped in and explained that I had been provided an academic tuition scholarship. Once my scholarship was confirmed, I was given only a bill for the dormitory room and board, which I mailed to my dad the next day.

I stopped back at the Student Union to purchase the books from my list, then lugged them back to the dorm for lunch. I felt pretty excited over my initial college experience, which wasn't so difficult or scary, after all!

Exploring

After lunch I ran into Larry again. We surveyed the neighborhood, confirming locations of the nearby liquor store, bar, grocery, Balaban & Katz movie theater,and various other shops. I noted a stationery store with typewriters in the window and planned to return when possible.

After dinner that evening, Father Joseph Small, S.J. (Society of Jesus), the Jesuit priest who ran the dormitory, held an orientation meeting in the first-floor lounge for all the residents. It looked like there were about 100 or 125 men in attendance. Father Small told us about the house rules: building curfew, no alcohol or women; overnight guests only by written permission. He told us about the laundry room, television lounge rules, cafeteria hours, and so forth.

Valuable Orientations

After the formal meeting, a group of upperclassmen gathered us freshman together for an additional orientation. They first told us about the Jesuit priests, disrespectfully called "Jebbies." These were the most intellectual of all the Catholic Orders, most holding PhD degrees, and tended to be the strictest teachers. They warned us that Father Small was likely to kick anyone out of the dorm who broke any of his rules, so we should be careful.

We asked about social life, meaning *girls*, and they said that the all-girl Mundelein College was on the far side of the Loyola campus, and many of the girls could be found on weekends in a small bar-nightclub near their campus. But they reminded us that these were all "good Catholic girls," likely virgins, and not very promising for freshmen carnal pursuits.

These upperclassmen told us that our North Shore neighborhood was called Rogers Park, a mostly Caucasian middle-class neighborhood, and the next town north on Sheridan Road was Evanston. We learned about the elevated train ("the El"), which runs from The Loop in downtown Chicago all the way to Evanston in the north. They told us about the fares, maps, nearby stations and schedules, usually every 15 minutes during the day and every 30 minutes at night. This chat was a really helpful education and orientation.

I asked about the ethnicity, since they had said ours was a "Caucasian middle-class" neighborhood, and they explained that Chicago-land neighborhoods tended to be divided vertically by ethnicity: there were German neighborhoods, Polish, Italian, Negro, Greek, and smaller groups of Ukrainians, Lithuanians, and Croatians. I found this unusual, because in Hawaii our neighborhoods were mostly divided horizontally, usually along economic lines, rich neighborhoods of all ethnicities and poor neighborhoods of all ethnicities. Back on Mauna Place, for example, most of our neighbors were well-to-do Chinese. But these guys explained that rich or poor, Germans usually lived in German neighborhoods, Poles in Polish neighborhoods, etc.

The next morning after breakfast Larry and I walked to school together, since we both had eight o'clock classes. Although we had similar class requirements, we never had the same instructors or schedules.

STERLING
Smith-Corona

II

To Keep My Scholarship

Serious Student

I felt my experience with English composition, speech, and German, provided me an academic advantage in at least those three courses. Knowing I'd lose my scholarship if I didn't get good grades, I settled in to become a very serious college student.

I took excellent notes, spent every evening assiduously studying at my desk, never frequented the TV lounge in the evening except for one hour a week to see *Gunsmoke*, a popular Western, starring my hero, Marshall Matt Dillon. My family had no home TV until I won one as a high school senior, so I really never got in the habit, and this TV indifference has been a lifelong benefit. I still don't own a TV set.

I devised a very strict schedule of at least one hour per class per night, and unfailingly stuck to it. Larry did pretty much the same, so we spent very quiet evenings working at our desks, while I drank instant coffee (I had a little electric coil which heated a cup of water) and smoked my Marlboro filter-tip cigarettes. Larry was one of a minority of male students who didn't smoke. He never complained, although I'm sure my smoking must have been annoying to him.

Larry was rather quiet and passive, and easy to get along with. Like the majority of men in the dorm, he left Friday afternoons for his nearby suburban home with his laundry in a box, to spend the weekend with his family. This left me alone in the room which was certainly pleasant. I had always been a kind of "loner," and enjoyed the seclusion until Larry returned with his box of clean laundry Sunday evening. I washed my own clothes on weekends in our dorm laundry room, and since my wardrobe consisted entirely of rumpled "wash and wear" cottons, it was an easy weekend chore.

Weekend Ritual

The cafeteria was closed after breakfast on Saturday until Monday morning, so I saved food from the previous week by collecting daily donuts and little boxes of cereal, as well as some fruit, which I kept in my room and lived on over the weekend. Six stale donuts, dry cereal, some wilted fruit, along with my instant coffee, was my rather monastic weekend diet. But on Sunday evenings Cindy Sue's across the street offered a special: Assuming it was pretty healthy, I feasted Sunday evening on bowls of tasty chicken livers.

I became a real "grind," spending my weekends in my room, reading and doing classwork. Never gave a thought to dating. Occasionally I'd go to the university library to look something up or check reference books. There was an ominous sign below the big library clock which read, TIME WILL PASS. WILL YOU?

Faithful Typewriter

On one Saturday morning, I revisited the stationery store I had seen earlier, purchased some envelopes, stamps, and note cards, and inspected their line of typewriters. My mother was writing to me every week and I was having to respond by hand, so I'd hoped to find something I could afford. They had a discounted "demonstrator" model of a high-quality Smith-Corona Portable Typewriter, which appeared to be just fine.

I asked what it meant to be a "demonstrator" and they explained that it had simply been tested by some customers in the store. It was not a "brand new" machine but retained the original guarantees. I recall it cost $45, which I paid in cash saved from last month's busboy job. (No such thing as a credit card then.)

It came with an extra ribbon and a very nice carrying case. I bought some packages of typing paper and carbon paper and brought my wonderful new possession back to the dorm. That manual typewriter (no electric typewriters for decades to come), faithfully served me at home for more than 30 years.

Two Quart Case

Later, I learned that the empty typewriter case could neatly hold two quarts of beer from the local liquor store. When I was asked for identification to prove I was not an 18-year- old college student, I had my reliable military photo-ID card proving John D. Kloppenburg was now 24-years-old. (I had acquired this lost ID card in high school and I resembled his ID photo, so it has proven valuable to me since then.) Sometimes I was asked for additional backup ID, and occasionally was refused service because I really did not look 24.

So I later got a Chicago library card in his name and I even went so far as to borrow a friend's car and took the state written and driving tests as John D. Kloppenburg, thus acquiring an Illinois driver's license as solid backup for the ID card. I later added a voter's card, so I had quite a collection, but the driver's license was the most valuable. The other cards I only used occasionally as additional backup.

Anyway, on some quiet Saturday nights in my room, I enjoyed bringing in a forbidden quart of beer to sip on while reading. (Although my typewriter case held two quarts, one quart sufficed for an evening, and I preferred to buy another cold quart some other night.) None of the student security at the front desk ever suspected, when I came in with a book under my arm and typewriter case in hand.

Chopped Fried Chicken Livers. All you can eat $2

Composition Struggle

As the months passed and quizzes and tests came along, I felt I was doing quite well in most of my courses. My major challenge was English Composition, with Professor Dion J. Wilhelmi. Each week he assigned a 500-word essay on some topic. Since I was pretty experienced with years of writing for essay contests, I felt I'd be able to "ace" this course. For the first assignment I tossed out something quick and easy and I got a D! I was stunned! It certainly wasn't A work, but it didn't deserve a D! On the next assignment, I put considerable effort into it and got a C minus! How could that be? I was upset and fearful for my grade point average (GPA). I knew that Larry was getting B's for what I felt were rather mediocre essays.

I searched out Dr. Wilhelmi and complained. He patiently explained, "John, you can do better ... much better. I've seen your high school records. You are an experienced speech and essay writer. I know you can do better. So, show me what you can do."

I came away flattered, yet disappointed. I needed extra study time for history and German, and had not planned to spend too much time on English Composition. But it looked like I wasn't going to have much choice. On the next assignment I put in a lot of time, editing and re-editing, and my essay was graded C+! This time I complained bitterly, but Wilhelmi wrote in the margin, "This is so much better! Keep it up, John."

It went this way for the rest of the semester. I worked harder and harder ... once got a B-, then later was rewarded by a B! But the highest grade I ever earned from him was a B+, and I feared that my final grade might be a C+ (averaging D to B+.) And how might that hurt my GPA? And my scholarship?

Lost Faith

Attending weekly Mass and Holy Communion was required all during high school, under the watchful eye of my father. Since graduation, with my travel to The Encampment for Citizenship in New York, and the summer job in Flossmoor, I had gotten out of the Sunday Mass habit. Once my school schedule was under control, I tried attending Mass on campus at Madonna Della Strada. Somehow, I no longer felt connected with the ritual and liturgy of Catholicism. After a few Sundays I stopped attending, drifted from Catholicism and embraced a more *spiritual* – rather than *religious* – outlook. I preferred spending my Sunday morning reading philosophy or anthropology.

I never had the opportunity to take a course in either anthropology or philosophy, but anthropology fascinated me and I read everything I could find time for. I loved learning how primitive *communication* (drums and smoke signals) led to *language*; or how man developed religion, music, art, cultural rituals, etc.

I loved *Semiotics*, the science of communication through signs and symbols. This includes symbolism and the meaning, interpretation, and understanding of these symbols. A kind of "visual rhetoric." Today's examples are traffic signals and lane markings, or icons designating restrooms, elevators, or handicap parking spaces.

My faithful non-electric companion for 40 years!

III

Polish Mafia

My Polish Mafia

Down the hall were two adjacent dorm rooms containing four friends. They were mostly Polish (and one Armenian), and had known one another in high school. There was Allen Zencka with Stan Kaczala, and "Swerk" Swierkowski with Charlie Osadjian. They were very fun and friendly, and "adopted" this Irishman. I called them "my Polish Mafia," and in succeeding years we developed a true brotherhood.

Clothing Bargain

By early October it was getting chilly in the "Windy City," and I needed a warm winter coat. Zencka and Kaczala told me the best buys in plain clothing could be had from the Jewish clothing merchants on Maxwell Street. If we arrived early in the day, we could get some real bargains.

So, the following Saturday we took the train down to the South edge of the city and walked the interesting Maxwell Street neighborhood, with all its clothing stores. In one store I found a nice hefty blue parka with a fur-lined hood. The price was $45, and it seemed very good quality. However, from the coaching by the boys, I declared the coat was too expensive and began to walk toward the door. The merchant pursued me, holding the parka, and said, "Take it for my price, $35!" I declined and kept moving away. Apparently, it's bad luck to lose the first customer of the day, so the guy complained, "You are stealing from me at $25, my very last offer!" I told him, "No, sorry," I lied, "I only have $15." Out on the sidewalk my companions began to cross the street and the merchant, coat in hand, chased us to the crosswalk saying, "$20, take it or leave it!" I offered $15 again, and in the middle of the crosswalk Alen gave him $3, so we settled at $18!

I felt a little guilty for behaving this way, but the guys assured me that this was perfectly proper etiquette, since both parties were satisfied. "So, what's the harm?" They insisted the merchant would have been offended if I didn't engage in back-and-forth negotiations. In fact, Allen said, "If you'd given him $45 in the beginning, he would probably not have taken it!" I loved that parka, which served me well for the next eight years I lived in Chicago.

Social Life

One Saturday night I thought it might be fun to go down to that bar near Mundelein College and check out those nice Catholic girls. Larry and my new friends had gone home for the weekend, as usual. I thought I'd be less shy with a companion, but there was none to be had, so I walked on over alone. I found the place, brightly lit, loud music, smoky, packed with boys and girls dancing and chatting at tables and the bar. I found a bar stool, ordered a beer, lit a cigarette, and enjoyed the music and watching all the couples dancing. I tried to start up a few conversations with unaccompanied young ladies, but my small talk seemed ineffective: as soon as they realized I was a *freshman*, living in the dorm, and without a car, they lost all interest. From the viewpoint of high school, a "college man" seemed to be quite a "big deal." But once on campus, a freshman was a very small frog in the big pond: these girls were surrounded by *upperclassmen* with apartments, cars, and even jobs (and *money*!).

So much for my college social life! I made no further attempts to meet a girl in that setting. It was cheaper and more fun at home in my room with a beer and a good book. Besides, very soon I'd be going home for Christmas break and spending time with my new girlfriend Shirley.

Slippah Merchant

In the dorm I always wore my Hawaiian "rubbah slippah" (rubber thong sandals), which at that time no one had ever seen, outside Hawaii or the Orient (the term for Asia then). All my friends wanted a pair, so I had my mother send me half a dozen pairs at a time. They cost her $1 a pair plus postage, and I sold them for $4; they became quite popular in the dorm. But they weren't always practical, as I later learned, wearing them out to the sidewalk mailbox, in the snow.

Postal Circle

My mom, who had been a sometime newspaper reporter and was a splendid touch-typist, wrote me a long, newsy, letter every week. With my wonderful new portable typewriter, I could respond weekly as well with a two-page, single-spaced letter, telling about school and friends and activities. The mail service was terrific: I would write my letter on Sunday, airmail it on Monday, and she received it in Honolulu on Wednesday. She would then write Wednesday evening, mail it on Thursday, and I'd receive her reply on Saturday. Then I could respond on Sunday, mail on Monday, and we continued this weekly "round trip" for several years. By the way, this was accomplished with a seven-cent *airmail* stamp each way.

Shirley sent this to keep on my desk. Pretty distracting!

Surprise!

Sixty years later, Mom presented me with a large old red suitcase of hers. Inside, I was surprised to find every one of the hundreds of letters I had written home during college and medical school. I had fun looking through some of them, and noticed that they were quite self-serving, telling how hard I was working, pinching my pennies, studying day and night, etc. Still, there were some interesting stories of various events. Dad also wrote me from his office, usually monthly, and often tucked in a $10 bill. My responses to his letters were also contained in this postal treasurer chest.

Sinful or Moral?

Not surprisingly, as we young males gathered for occasional evening "bull sessions" in the dorm, the subject would often turn to sex. The culture was very different then, and like most high school grads, and virtually all Catholic teens, we were inexperienced. Even the "mechanical" aspects of sexual intercourse were shrouded in mystery. There was no Internet pornography at the time, so none of us had actually seen any sex act. Our knowledge of female anatomy was limited to glances at topless natives in National Geographic, or the occasional, and quite stirring, *Playboy* magazine "foldouts" that someone might pilfer from an uncle or an older brother.

In our more thoughtful moments, we also considered, but rarely spoke of, the concept of sexual "sin," and specifically the mortal sin of "premarital sex." Our priests had frightened us with eternal hellfire simply for masturbating; what might be the horrible punishment for forbidden sexual activity?

Some of us had girlfriends, but they were invariably chaste Catholic virgins also, and not likely to change their minds. So we had no "inside knowledge" to contribute. Thus, the *sinfulness* of intimacy, although of profound interest, was purely academic, at least for the immediate future.

With my rejection of Catholic dogma, I had abandoned the concept of sin, but with my newfound interest in spirituality, my concerns were about the morality of our actions. I adopted a pragmatic approach to the morality issue: if two mature adults consented to engage in any legal behavior, how could that be immoral? The only immorality would arise by proceeding without one's consent, or if forced, or dishonestly acquired.

It all seemed very reasonable and moral – but I wondered if my pragmatic philosophy was an excuse to justify my own sexual desires. However, it didn't much matter since I had no partner to offer her consent anyway

IV

The Turning Point

The Cat Dissector

One night, walking down the hall to the shower, I smelled a familiar odor – like formaldehyde – in the hallway. This time it was stronger than usual and seemed to be coming from one of the rooms with an open door. Curious, I leaned in. The room was dark, but I could see a guy hunched over something on his desk, illuminated only by his desk lamp.

"Come in," he called.

"I was just looking for the smell," I said.

"Oh," he replied, "Sorry, that's the formalin. I should keep the door shut, but I wanted to air-out the room."

"Formalin? In your room? What are you doing?" I asked.

"It's my cat," he said. "It's our homework."

I came in, and as I got closer, I could see by the desk lamp, there on a wax dissection tray, was the body of a dead cat! The cat's belly and chest were split wide open, and I could see two tiny kittens in each side of her Y-shaped (bicornuate) uterus. It was simply amazing: the fascinating parts of this preserved cat in a dorm room!

"*Homework?* What's this all about?" I asked.

"This is part of our class in Comparative Anatomy. Last month we dissected a pigeon and next month we'll do a little Dogfish shark. Each month we dissect a new animal. The course is part of the Pre-Med Curriculum."

Then he showed me, "Here are her lungs," and when he gently pressed on them, he could create a kind of meow sound!

"And here is her heart," he went on. "And this is her liver." It was all so beautifully organized!

He had a cat anatomy guidebook on the desk and a small set of dissection instruments. I found all this completely amazing and absolutely fascinating, to see all these neatly arranged parts, and I told him so.

"If you're interested, you should *audit* the course next semester. If you audit it, you pay tuition and can attend all the classes, and do all the labs like this if you wish, and you don't have to take any exams, but no credit. You might enjoy it, and have a lot of fun!"

We spoke for a few more minutes and I became very excited about learning something new like this. At early registration for next semester, I dropped Psychology 102 or something, and signed-up to audit this lecture/lab biology course. Little did I know it at the time, but this conversation proved, literally, to be *life changing*. *Providential?*

USOA

I continued my compulsive studying through the fall, while corresponding with Shirley and looking forward to Christmas vacation in Hawai'i. My dad contacted Angie Rossi, my former boss at KIKI, and for $100 was able to buy some USOA airline "comp tickets" i.e., *complimentary*, which Rossi had received as payment for radio advertising. USOA (United States Overseas Airlines) was a *non-sched* ("Nonscheduled Air Carrier"), which flew only when it had a full load of passengers. The service was irregular, and the airline operated from out-of-the-way California airports, such as Burbank and Oakland. The service was so inconvenient that some joked that the USOA initials stood for "Use Some Other Airline." Despite the unpredictability and inconvenience, the tickets were quite economical, so were always my thrifty father's first choice.

Straight A!

I studied hard through the fall and crammed for finals after Thanksgiving. Exams were in early December. I was elated, and not a little surprised, that I had *six A's* on my report card! Even an A from Dr. Wilhelmi, my English Comp instructor, who had never given me more than a B! But by withholding good essay grades, he made me a better writer. *Thanks, Professor!*

I was so excited that I sent my parents a brief telegram: *"Hooray straight A's!"* My parents later said that since telegrams usually marked deaths or disasters, they were almost afraid to open it. But they were thrilled, and this guaranteed renewal of my scholarship. And big savings for my thrifty parents.

Winter

December in Chicago – my first in twelve years – was mighty cold, with freezing winds blowing across Lake Michigan. My big blue parka was a blessing: the furry hood spared my ears from freezing, but I had forgotten how cold my nose could become. I sure couldn't wait for my trip home to Hawaii.

There were barely two weeks available for Christmas vacation at home, so I didn't try to get a radio job. Rob gave me back my Hudson Hornet so I could get around. I spent days tanning and playing on the beach with Shirley Rollinson, a beautiful, delightful Sacred Hearts Academy Senior.

Soon it was time to take a non-sched midnight USOA flight back to some inconvenient California airport where I could later connect with a real airline back to Chicago.

Enjoying the beach with Shirley, chaperoned by Mom "Sunny," and sister, Carol.

V

Second Semester

Spring '57

This spring semester I began the 102 versions of most of the fall courses, although with different instructors, as well as my new audit course, Comparative Anatomy. I was thinking of my intended career in *communication*: broadcasting, advertising, and public relations. Back in the dorm Larry and I were still rooming together. I needed a little spending money and didn't want to ask my parents, since they were paying the dorm fees, so I went looking for a part time job.

Car Job

I found a convenient after-school job at Broadway Lincoln-Mercury, just a few blocks down Sheridan Road. I worked after classes from 3 till 6 weekday afternoons, detailing cars, washing, polishing, etc., and doing janitorial work in the offices. This provided me with the requisite spending money for cigarettes and the occasional weekend meal or beer, since my dating life was non-existent.

The first few months of my job were difficult, because my hands suffered from washing cars outdoors in the freezing weather. Gloves weren't much help. The work became more tolerable as the spring warmed up. I enjoyed detailing the new '57 models as they arrived for sale.

Grandma's Dinner

My Grandma Lavinia was still living in Chicago and I had not seen her since her last visit to Honolulu. One weekend she invited me to dinner at her apartment in the Seneca Hotel, where she had lived alone for the past 30 or more years. The hotel had been converted to studio apartments with kitchenette, much more convenient for her. We had a nice dinner of scallops and a vegetable. She said, "This is what I have every night." (This was the truth: whenever I came for dinner in future years, the meal was always identical!)

Earlier photo of Grandma in her office running her very successful executive secretary training school, surrounded by appreciative photos of business titans.

She told me of her very successful Corboy Personnel Service business, which provided her a good income to live her life in a fine hotel. She said that she had retired and sold the company to Mrs. Calvin and the name was now Corboy-Calvin Personnel Service. She declared that it was a shame that Mrs. Calvin couldn't maintain the *quality* of the management and training of the clients. It was nice to catch up with Grandma, and she seemed to be in pretty good physical and mental health for someone in their eighties.

I admired her gutsy independence and entrepreneurial spirit. At a time when divorce was rare and women were usually homemakers, she had left her Indiana husband, moved to Chicago, created her own business training women as executive secretaries, and found her graduates were in great demand. She served all the notable executives in Chicagoland and surrounding states. "Hard work always wins," she loved to say. I guess some of that philosophy rubbed-off on me.

Business Lesson

That spring, my dad's brother, Uncle Steve, an attorney who worked for the big Simonize Company, invited me for a Saturday drive to their *Ivalon* Sponge Factory in nearby Benton Harbor, Michigan. Steve explained that a few years ago he had met with a Czech chemist who had developed a crude *artificial sponge*. Steve realized the value, since at the time, sponges were all natural sea sponges. He wrote the patents, then convinced Simonize to buy the rights and bring the inventor to Chicago to work on developing and improving the sponges. Soon the development team had created a finely-porous, long-lasting *synthetic* sponge. They named it *Ivalon*, and their sponges became very popular, making lots of money for the company and a big bonus for Steve.

At the factory, Steve showed me two huge vats of a yellow soupy material that would become the sponges. He explained that one vat contained the pure chemical, which provided very long-lasting sponges which were sold to the government for use in the military.

"This other vat contains the domestic sponges. The formula is adulterated with acid to weaken the chemical bonds, so the sponges don't last as long."

This seemed strange: they produced both a superior product and an inferior one. Steve explained that there was no money in a very long-lasting consumer product. He pulled out his pack of cigarettes and said, "When will I buy another pack, Johnny? When the cigarettes are all gone. It's the same with the sponges: the housewife will buy another one only when her sponge gives out. And even our inferior-quality sponge is better and lasts longer than anything else on the market, so consumers are quite happy with it. There's no money, Johnny, in a consumer product that lasts forever."

This was an interesting lesson in business. But it still seemed somewhat unusual to sell an inferior product, knowing that it could be improved upon. But I could understand the idea of consumption.

HISTORICAL NOTE

Hawaiian Fun: In the '50s, Hawai'i was a little-known territory to mid-westerners, with relatively few tourists. Many of my dorm friends wondered whether my family lived in grass huts, what we did for money, if we spoke Hawaiian, and whether all girls wore hula skirts.

I assured them that we had been living in a grass hut but recently my father was building us a real house. I explained that we used traditional shell-money but were considering adopting the US dollar. I told them it had been a challenge to learn Hawaiian and when they asked for a sample. I rattled off:

> "Ua Mau ke Ea o ka āina i ka Pono" (State Motto), "Ha'ina 'ia mai ana ka puana" (Song Refrain), "Waikīkī Ewa Mauka Makai" (Directions), "Humuhumunukunukuapua'a" (State Fish), "Wai'anae Nānākuli No Ka Oi Mele Kalikimaka Puka Pants!"

These phrases were mostly gibberish; we lived in real houses, spoke English almost exclusively, used the US dollar, and wore hula skirts for only dancing the hula.

Pre-Med Pals

The best fun of this semester was my new class in Comparative Anatomy: it was just as fascinating as I had expected it to be, and I really enjoyed my classmates, all of whom were in the Loyola Pre-Med Curriculum.

This Curriculum was a challenging program which provided students – in four years – the requisite 120 hours of science needed to apply to medical school: eight semesters of 15 science hours each.

I learned that for 20 science hours *every* semester, the stout-hearted could manage the 120 hour goal in six semesters, or just three college years! The courses were famously tough: the Loyola Pre-Med Curriculum overall dropout rate was as high as 50%, and it was not easy to maintain a satisfactory GPA.

Many of my classmates lived in the dorm, and the upperclassmen even gave me guidance in my desktop dissections. I loved the way the animals' internal organs were so neatly organized, just like they were in the anatomy book. I also enjoyed some stimulating conversations with several of the pre-med upperclassmen regarding their Curriculum. While they all agreed the courses were really challenging, they understood the need, and shared a joy and fascination with all the science they were learning. I found them all smart, personable, earnest, and inspired by the opportunity for a career in medicine.

VI

Career Questions

Unexpected Attraction

One of my classmates, Marty Shafer, encouraged me to consider a switch to the pre-med program: "Corboy, since you enjoy all this dissection stuff, maybe you should become a surgeon and you can dissect people," he joked.

The idea was an intriguing one: my father was a physician, though he had never encouraged me in that direction, and I admired how he cared for patients and really enjoyed his work helping them. What I knew of the Pre-Med Curriculum seemed quite interesting – although intimidating – and my dorm pre-med classmates were all fine fellows: smart, kind, and helpful.

But what of my intended career in broadcasting, public relations, and advertising? (Together, these are classified as *Communication*, and had led me to an appreciation of *semiotics*.)

If I switched and began the Pre-Med Curriculum in the coming fall semester, it'd be in the beginning of my sophomore year. If I could manage to complete the 120-hour program in just *three* years, I would graduate in the normal four years of college. But if I couldn't handle the three-year load of 20 science hours per semester, and had to do a fourth pre-med year, I'd be doing five years of college with associated expenses for my family.

Bright Idea

Yet my pre-med pals were having such fun learning all this science: lectures and laboratories in biology, embryology, chemistry, anatomy, physics, physiology, organic chemistry, and bio-statistics and more. In talking with them late at night I became excited by *their* enthusiasm, and my thoughts began focusing on a career in medicine. Maybe I actually *could* do it, and become a *doctor*, no matter how many semesters it took!

And to think that this new career dream all began with a bad smell in the dorm hallway, that led me to meet *the cat dissector!* Sure seems like *Providence!*

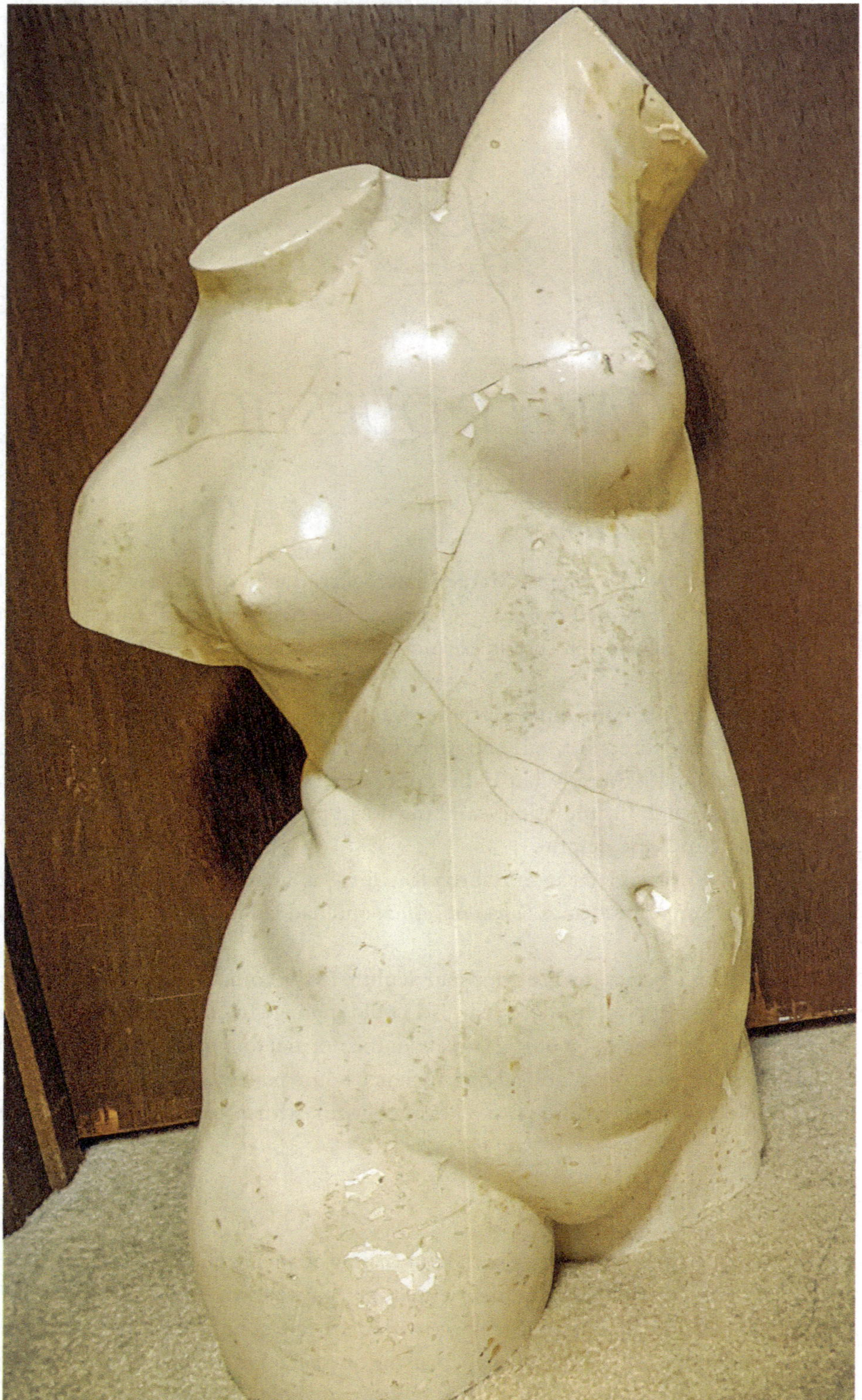

Still faithful after all these years!

VII

An Impossible Dream?

New Career Plan

Yearning now for a possible career in medicine, yet reluctant to prolong my college years longer than necessary, I came up with a dream of acquiring all those 120 science hours *within just two years*, rather than an admittedly stressful three, or the normal four years. Plowing my way through the catalogues of required pre-med science courses, I found that by combining night school and possibly summer school for the coming four semesters, I could almost reach the required number of hours. To do this, I needed to inappropriately juggle the schedule where I might have to take courses at night or out of order, such as taking *qualitative* chemical analysis within the same semester as *quantitative* chemical analysis, where the first was supposed to *precede* the second.

Long Shot

I expected that this unique schedule would be difficult to pull off, because Loyola Pre-Med Curriculum protocols seemed pretty rigid. But I knew if I could get approval, perhaps from the Dean, I just might be able to make it happen. I neatly typed up a schedule of courses for the next four semesters. This was 30 science lecture and lab hours per semester, including night school. I listed none for summer school, which would be a backup in case I had failed one or another course.

I promptly took my plan to the Dean, Father Hartnett, S.J., for his approval. He seemed uncertain about some of the course registration rules. Then he checked my file, shrugged, and said, "This looks awfully strenuous, son. But I see you've done well so far; if you can handle it, it's OK with me."

Brilliant Thought!

I thanked him, and as a brilliant afterthought, asked Father to *sign his approval.* He hesitated for a moment, then scribbled his name on my proposed curriculum sheet. Elated, I went back to the dorm thinking that *Providence* was helping me make an impossible dream come true. The rest would be up to me – and my diligence.

My evening conversations with some of the pre-med upperclassmen were much more exciting now. I was following in their footsteps as a hopeful *pre-med student*. Some of them kidded me that Night School classes were not part of the formal Curriculum and were probably with the nursing students, mostly girls, and were likely easier courses than those in the daytime Pre-Med Curriculum. Well, that wasn't my purpose, but I wouldn't mind a little help with my GPA. And who knows, I might even meet a girl!

I told a friend of my two-year plan.

"Three or four years work in two? You're nuts! It's gonna be really tough. Nothing but science courses! And you won't get a degree. I don't think they will let you do it," he said.

I told him of the Dean's approval.

"Well, you won't have much fun because it would be 120 hours of only science, and you may not be able to keep up your GPA with *30 science hours per semester!* That's such a heavy load! Besides, since your courses will be all science, you'll miss those other required courses needed for a BS in Biology."

"But I'm not here for *fun*," I replied. I reasoned that if I could get into Graduate School, whatever degree I earned there would be more valuable than the bachelor's degree I'd get from Loyola by enrolling for an additional year. So I would just have to do my best to make the "impossible dream" come true.

Marty said, "One step at a time, pal; first, let's see if you can even get through pre-registration next month."

Black Friday

Late Friday afternoon April 26, they called me down to the dorm front office for a *long-distance* phone call. These usually signified some kind of disaster, so my heart sank a bit when I picked up the phone. It was Virginia Brodhead, a lady friend in Honolulu, who cried out, "Nancy's dead!"

"What, Nancy Phillips, my former girlfriend and sweet pal?

Ginny, I can't believe it! What happened?"

"It was a car crash," she sobbed. "Four Punahou senior girls on Spring Break in a rainstorm up near Punalu'u. Three were killed when they went off the road. I'll mail you the clipping from yesterday's *Star-Bulletin*." She gave me a few more details, but it just seemed unbelievable. Nancy was smart, lovely, talented, and with a beautiful soul.

I loved Nancy and treasured the wonderful romantic times we had together. It was my first experience with death of a loved one. I took it pretty hard: I went across the street to the liquor store, where John Kloppenburg bought a pint of whiskey for me, and I went down to sit on the lake shore at sunset to "drown my sorrows."

"Thanks, Nancy, for all the joy."

Car Job

I was enjoying my work at Broadway Lincoln-Mercury more now that the weather was warming, and washing cars outdoors was not so unpleasant. I told them I'd be leav-

Weather Forecast

Honolulu Star-Bulletin

Note, Subscribers:

Honolulu Star-Bulletin, Vol. 46, No. 99 Phone 5-7911 HONOLULU, TERRITORY OF HAWAII, U. S. A. THURSDAY, APRIL 25, 1957 HOME EDITION 10¢

3 Punahou Coeds Die in Wreck On Kam Highway; 4th Girl Hurt

Late Evening Crash at Punaluu Snuffs Out Lives of Senior Trio

Officer Maxwell Komaiopili examines the accident car

Judith

Nancy Jean Phillips

Katherine Ann Chapin

Brenda Lee Parsons

Special Services Are Planned for Girls

U.S. Fleet Ordered to Middle East; Jordan Premier Is Forced to Resign

(Courtesy of **Honolulu Star-Advertiser** *archives)*

ing for the summer, but happy to return in the fall, although with shorter hours if I could get the new class schedule I hoped for. The new Edsel models had been arriving; they were quite nice, but sales were mixed.

Stranger on a Train

The preceding summer when I was on the train to New York for my summer with the Encampment for Citizenship (EFC), a fellow seatmate, a college guy, told me about his adventures in France with The Experiment in International Living.

He said the organization had been started before World War II, in the hope that students who had lived in foreign countries would appreciate the culture and language, make many friends, and in later life would not want to go to war with those countries. A great concept, but not in time to prevent World War II. However, the program blossomed in the post-war years and was becoming very popular with students.

The guy said he chose France from among several possible countries, and traveled

Father Small felt "Venus" was "lewd."

in a group of ten Americans with a French-speaking American leader. He and each of his fellow students lived with a family who had youngsters of about the same age. He explained that after an extended homestay, the group traveled throughout France with their family's youngsters, and it had been his life's greatest adventure! It sounded exciting, so I wrote for informational materials and an application.

Registration Challenge

In May, I went to preregistration for the coming '57 fall semester. I plowed through the boxes of the usual IBM registration cards, collecting those on my course list, and brought them to a supervisor. He carefully studied the cards, then laughed and said, "Sorry son, you can't do this. You can't take this biology at night and you can't do *qual chem* in the same semester as *quant chem*. And 15 science hours per semester is fine. 20 hours is more than enough; but 30 hours is *way too much!* Now put these cards back and let's do it *by the book*."

Success!

At this point I produced my four-semester program and showed him that my plan was approved by Father Hartnett. He looked surprised, scratched his head, and said, "Well, if it's OK with the Dean, it's OK with me. I don't think it'll work, but good luck!" *Hallelujah!*

So next semester would be jammed with all-science lectures and labs. I'd have to cut back on my after-school job to manage the afternoon labs, but at least I had gotten this far. I was so excited! I was now an unofficial pre-med student with my own *approved* science curriculum. Most of my courses were with the regular pre-med group, but night classes, like that biology 102, were not.

Venus

One Saturday a few of my "Polish Mafia" pals took me along with them to a nearby furniture and antique store. I think one of the guys wanted to get some furniture for his dorm room, perhaps a foot stool or something. I was intrigued by a beautiful female torso sculpture. The storekeeper said she was an original, created in an art class, and pointed out the straw within her armature. I didn't care about her origin. I thought she was beautiful! I decided she would make a nice roommate for a guy with no social life. I brought "Venus" home and put her proudly on my bookshelf.

Venus was on proud display for a mere two weeks before Father Small announced that she was "lewd and unacceptable," or words to that effect. (Did he inspect our rooms while we were in class?) I fibbed and told him that she was a gift of "fine art from my grandmother," but he didn't care. I was ordered to put Venus in the closet and take her home when I left for the summer. I wrapped her in a blanket in the back of the closet, letting her remain in Chicago. Venus was no longer seen in the dorm, but she has since accompanied me for sixty-five years in eight residences, longer than any of my lady friends, and nicer than many.

My favorite photo of the loving couple.

VIII

*B*USY SUMMER

Summer '57

My 3.6 GPA (down from 4.0) indicated that in this second semester I had done a few other things besides studying. Nevertheless, it was sufficient to maintain my scholarship. Soon it was time for another USOA economy flight home for the summer. Shirley and I had been corresponding heavily since Christmas. She had just graduated from Sacred Hearts Academy and we couldn't wait to get together again.

Dairy Guy

Dad had arranged with a patient of his, Paul Heckenlively, the manager of Foremost Dairy, to give me a job assisting in the Dairy's laboratory. This was 7am to 3pm daily. The dairy work was really interesting and educational.

Lovely couple: I wonder where we were going?

Milk Processing

Early in the morning, the first tanker trucks of "raw" (unpasteurized) milk arrived from local dairy farms. These tankers were first weighed, then I climbed atop. I took a sample of the milk from deep in the center of the tank with a container on a long pole, then carried the sample to the lab for measurement of bacterial count and butterfat content. The tanker was then drained and weighed again. This gave us the net weight of raw milk delivered. Unscrupulous dairymen might add water to their tank to increase the weight of milk delivered, in order to increase their payment. However, this could be self-defeating, since payment depended on the butterfat content (the higher the better), which would be reduced by added water. If the fat content was too low, or bacterial count too high, the milk might be refused. "Whole Milk" (4%) was prized; this was before the days of low-fat and "skim" milk.

Lab Work

After pasteurizing, flavoring, coloring and packaging, I would choose samples from a daily list of random items off the production line for testing. For example, for ice cream, it might be a quart of vanilla, a pint of chocolate, and a half-gallon of Neopolitan. In the lab we would incubate a sample of each in Petri dishes to test for coliform bacterial counts, and another sample of each was tested for butterfat content. We also tested various milk products, such as whole and skim milk, buttermilk, as well as cream and half-and-half.

My boss, Mr. Erickson, kept careful track of all the results, so that any problems were caught early and reported to foremen and management. Since I was now a science major at school, it was great fun to be learning about Dairy Science.

In the middle of the summer a union organizer came around and told management that since this was a union shop, as an employee I needed to become a dues-paying union member. Mr. Heckenlively argued that I was merely a part-time, "temporary hire." I believe the issue was settled when I returned to school in the fall.

Freebie

A great benefit of this job was that we lab workers were expected to dispose of the sampled containers of ice cream and other products. We could trash them, or we could take them home. Our home freezer soon bulged with great Foremost Ice Cream, which became a staple of our summer meals.

Radio Guy

I wanted to keep in touch with broadcasting, and I found a great job at KGU, something called *Roadshow* for the afternoon traffic audience, with a charming co-host, Muriel Waters. We covered the 3 to 6 pm "rush hour" and by zooming from the dairy, I could usually get to the studio before 3:30.

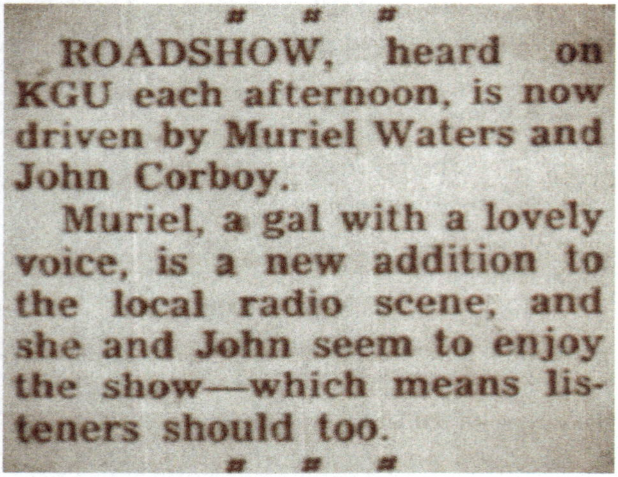

\# \# \#

ROADSHOW, heard on KGU each afternoon, is now driven by Muriel Waters and John Corboy.

Muriel, a gal with a lovely voice, is a new addition to the local radio scene, and she and John seem to enjoy the show—which means listeners should too.

\# \# \#

Story about our popular show.
(Courtesy** Honolulu Star-Advertiser **Archives.)

Responding to my earlier request for a broadcast opportunity, my high school KIKI broadcast friend, Johnny DeMarco, now station manager at KPOA, offered me a job from 7 to 10 pm weekday evenings, playing the top 40 pop music. I barely had time after KGU at 6 pm for a quick bite, but this pop format was very popular and fun, and I loved chatting with callers. For some reason, Johnny assigned me the disc jockey name "Jonathan Knight." And so I was.

My parents were surprised that I took on *both* these after-work jobs, but broadcasting is addictive, and I wanted to keep in touch with my radio pals. I usually left the house at 6:30am and got home at 10:30 in the evening. Some vacation! But I loved it!

Contacts

I don't know how we worked it in – maybe on Saturdays – but my dad's friend, AO dealer Bob Miller fitted me with the very novel *contact lenses*. At the time they were hard PMMA plastic, and very scratchy and uncomfortable at first. But once I got used to them, I was comfortable and happy to see – and to be seen – without glasses. I became a happy hard-lens wearer for the next twenty years.

Romance

Unfortunately, my time with Shirley was limited to weekends, but we certainly made the best use of our time, beaching by day, with evening movies or parties with friends. It was all very sweetly romantic (sticking to that "no touching below the neck" high school rule), and we began talking about a future together.

Valuable Advice

I remember having dinner with Don Chamberlain, my high school radio mentor and idol, and told him of my considering a switch to the pre-med program, versus continuing my plans for a career in broadcasting, advertising, and public relations. I wanted his opinion.

"You *must* take the pre-medical program, Laddy! I want you to become a doctor. You've got real talent for broadcasting, as well as terrific radio experience at your age; you've got a great future in broadcasting. But you can do more good, and I think be more satisfied, as a doctor. This radio stuff is all ego and fun, but pretty trivial. You can make a real difference in people's lives as a doc."

This surprisingly strong opinion from someone I really trusted and admired, who knew our shared love of radio, really got my attention; this certainly helped me to feel that I was making the right decision. I became determined to put all my best efforts into the coming semester.

Thanks, Don!

Cowboys!

Before heading back to school, I quit all my jobs to spend a week hosting Allen Zencka. He had never been to the Islands, so flew in for a week's visit before school started. We first toured Oahu, then flew to Kauai for a day and rented a U-Drive car, which we slept in to economize.

Then to Maui, for a pre-arranged three-day horseback trip through a dormant volcano, the magnificent Haleakala Crater, with the renowned Makawao cowboy, Frank Freitas. We rode all day through the colorful lava floor of the enormous crater, camping each night in one of the three rustic cabins. Frank woke us each morning with a big mug of fresh black coffee, and gave us the same mug at bedtime filled with red wine! He always enjoyed the same, explaining it was for "All us *Portagee* (Portuguese) *Cowboys*." The excitement came when we raced after Frank as he galloped off, chasing a goat over the rocky terrain! Occasionally, he was actually able to lasso the fleeing critter and we were impressed that they smelled absolutely awful! Whew!

Saddle sore and weary, we flew back to Honolulu, and Allen went on to Chicago.

I kissed Shirley and my family goodbye: it was time for another USOA flight to California. The flights were still just $100, but I could see why these cheap, "non-scheds" were unpopular. My promised flight was delayed two days (awaiting a full load) before flying to California. Little wonder people joked that USOA meant "Use Some Other Airline."

Fall '57

Back in the dorm, my new roommate, Tom Conway, had already moved in. I think Larry Kaufman had had enough of my cigarette smoking and decided to change roommates. He had been a great "roomie" for my first year. Tom was also a smoker, so we really stunk up the room!

My dearest friend, "big brother", and mentor Don Chamberlain.

Lovely lei on departure for school.

IX

"IMPOSSIBLE" SCHEDULE

Grueling

My new course schedule was certainly grueling, since the pre-med courses were so tough. It was a long day with the extra labs I had entered in my afternoon schedule. Then came the evening course, biology 102, with Dr. Benedict Jaskowski, a very pleasant teacher and parasite researcher. The course was lighter than the daytime pre-med version, since it was for the pre-nursing students. Within a few weeks I had befriended a lovely redhead named Sue Whitson. It wasn't long before I talked her into coming home to "See my dorm room" after classes.

Fun Mischief

Women were strictly prohibited from the dormitory, so I met Sue at the back door freight entrance with a laundry cart I'd secured from the utility room. She hopped into the cart, I lay a sheet over her, and rolled Sue up to my room. Tom had obligingly stepped out, to read or watch tv in the lounge. Sue and I thought we were so very clever and we enjoyed an hour of hugging, kissing, and beer. Nothing more intimate, being good Catholic virgins. I later rolled her back to the exit, and on the way we encountered a couple of students who wondered what I was doing with the cart. I explained that I "had a little accident" and had needed to change my sheets.

We repeated this clandestine, platonic dating a couple more times, despite the risk of expulsion, but by semester's end I'd lost interest in the lack of intimacy.

Thanks, Sue!

Independents' Fraternity

There were several national fraternities represented on campus, but most dorm people weren't interested in fraternity house living and spent their weekends at home in nearby suburbs. The pre-meds, with their heavy schedules also felt that frat house living simply was not conducive to long study hours. However, my "Polish Mafia" friends

My new roommate, Tom Conway, at his colorful desk.

Charlie Osadjian and Stan Kaczala admired the fraternity jackets worn by many fellow students and decided that we should have our own little "dormitory fraternity," just for the five of us. They chose ΓΔΙ (Gamma Delta Iota) symbolizing our independence: GDI (God Damned Independents).

The jackets they ordered were beautiful: red and black woolen, embroidered with our Greek letters, and with white leather sleeves. We really looked sharp, just like *real* fraternity guys.

Some Pranks

Studying hard with very little social activity, it seemed we were all filled with a certain amount of stressful energy. A couple of pranks seemed to "let off a little steam."

Scorpion Surprise

Father Small was universally unpopular and most of the dorm guys thought he was unnecessarily strict and dictatorial. (Not to mention that he'd prohibited my lovely Venus sculpture!) My friends decided on a prank to annoy him: they collected a couple dozen crayfish from a fish market and made a sign "Scorpions to the Scorpion." Late that night they built a little cardboard barrier outside his door, then put the dozens of crayfish scuttling within, up against his door. Then they propped up the sign so it could be easily seen, hoping he would mistake the crayfish for scorpions as they scuttled into his room when he opened his door. No one was able to witness the event the following morning, but he certainly must have been startled. Father Small resigned management of the dormitory at year's end.

Buffalo Surprise

Here's another prank: one night a few of us were taking a rare after-dinner walk in a nearby neighborhood. In a front yard we noticed a full-size stuffed buffalo behind a low picket fence. It was secured by wires to tie-downs in the ground, so that it wouldn't fly away or be carried off. Someone (maybe me?) suggested that it might be great fun to actually *steal* the buffalo. Although we had no idea what we would want to do with it, it seemed like a fun prank to pull off.

I guess I was chosen as the leader for this nonsense, because I secured a pair of wire cutters and Swerkowski's pickup truck. We planned to hop the little fence, slice the wires, and four of us would lift the buffalo into the truck.

So, one night we pulled up outside the house, and I hopped over the fence with my wire cutters. Suddenly the porch light came on, the door burst open, and the homeowner popped out holding a flashlight, shouting at me, "What the hell do you boys think you're doing?"

Caught in the act! It was so embarrassing! I mumbled something stupid, like, "Sorry, wrong house," but he started laughing – then my friends on the sidewalk started laughing – *at me*! It turned out that my pals thought the theft was a bad idea, so they had earlier advised the homeowner, who was waiting for us. So the joke was on me! *Thanks guys!*

Job Offer

My Student Counselor called me in one day, and asked if I were related to Lavinia Corboy. I said, "Yes, she's my grandmother." He replied that he knew of her, and her very popular Corboy Personnel Service. I hadn't realized her business was so well known.

Anyway, he had invited me in, to ask if I'd be interested in a job at the Institute for Juvenile Research (IJR). It was a live-in, room and board, and salary opportunity as a boys' counselor/peacekeeper. He said, "Your grades are good, and I think you can handle an off-campus job." I was flattered and thanked him, but explained that my new class schedule wouldn't permit working off-campus. And maintaining discipline among a bunch of "juvenile delinquents" didn't sound very appealing!

Experiment Application

I had received the requested informational materials from The Experiment in International Living, which were quite fascinating. Since German was my only foreign language, I applied for a trip to Germany the next summer. I noticed that some scholarships were available, so I applied for financial aid, as well. Can't hurt!

All-Science Course Load

This first semester with my heavy pre-med science load (30 hours, instead of 15 or 20), had proven really challenging, especially those long afternoon labs. But I was super-compulsive, and determined to do well in every one of my courses. I recall having so many things to do for each course, that I had a "to do" list for each one. And just to keep track of these, I made *a list of all my lists*! But it worked well, and I was proud of my pre-med grades so far.

X

EXCITING CHRISTMAS BREAK

Worm Job?

At semester's end, my biology professor, Dr Jaskowski, offered me a job in his lab the following semester. He was doing some fascinating work with *Ascaris Lumbricoides*, a parasitic roundworm which infected pigs. He was studying the life cycle in pigs, searching for ways to prevent or halt the infestations. The worms could completely occlude the intestinal tracts of pigs, sickening or killing them. This illness was of great economic importance in the pork industry. I thanked him for the opportunity, and was pleased by his confidence in me, but unsure if I could manage the time.

The semester ended, and it was time for a short Christmas trip home. I was eager to see Shirley, and it was my brother Rob's last semester at Punahou.

Christmas '57

As always, my first thought was to get a radio job. At KGU I found an opportunity as a "holiday coverage" guy, filling in for staffers on a Christmas break. We had special programming, mostly music during Christmas week, so Owen Cunningham, the classical music emcee, had chosen a large selection of long-playing (33⅓) Christmas albums, mostly chorale and instrumental European carols, before he left on vacation. I loved these old English, French, and German carols, playing them by the hour, and learning European Christmas customs and history.

I also covered for the morning shift engineer, which included running the board for the Lucky Luck morning-drive show. My job was to call Lucky at 4 am to get him in for his 5 to 9 am broadcast. Lucky was a beloved character, chattering in pidgin, but he was often at least an hour late and pretty hung over. It was a challenge to manage his show in his absence.

Occasionally I also assisted Joe Rose when he did "re-created" baseball games, usually the popular minor league San Francisco Seals. In these broadcasts, using only a box-score sheet off the teletype, Joe could describe the action as if he were there in the

This little guy inspired me all the way. And he still does!

Still Love Her, Chamberlain Says

Disc Jockey Survives Flurry of Shots As Distraught Wife Climaxes Quarrel

Don Chamberlain, radio disc jockey, said today he still loves his wife even though she took five pistol shots at him during a domestic quarrel last night.

Back at his usual early morning job behind KGMB's microphone, Chamberlain told radio listeners his wife is expecting a child and said other mothers would understand how upset a wcman becomes at such a time.

The Chamberlains also have 15-month-old twin daughters.

Construction noises next door and humid weather contributed to his wife's outburst, he said.

Chamberlain explained that his wife is a good pistol shot and was perfectly capable of hitting him if she wanted.

Don Chamberlain

He stood still as his wife fired a .22 calibre automatic at him from nine feet away, police reported.

Chamberlain said he knows now it was a mistake to keep a gun in the house.

It was just a normal domestic quarrel, he said, and if there hadn't been a pistol around, his wife would have thrown some chinaware and the incident never would have made headlines.

Chamberlain said one listener had called to criticize him for not being home with his family today. "We've got to eat," he said, by way of explaining his presence at work.

DOMESTIC QUARREL

The shooting at 9:20 p.m. climaxed an evening of bickering about a personal matter in the Chamberlains' apartment at 2990-D Kalakaua Avenue.

One bullet buried itself in the sofa, one hit the floor in front of him, and three thudded against the wall but didn't go through.

Mrs. Chamberlain, visibly shaken, slumped to a chair and dropped the pistol.

A neighbor heard the shots and called police. Mrs. Chamberlain, emotionally upset, was taken to Queen's Hospital. No charges were filed.

★ ★ ★

50,000 Guns Registered Since '22, Police Say

At least 50,000 guns have been registered with the Honolulu Police Department since 1922, Records Captain Neil A. Donahue said today.

"There's no way of telling how many of these are still in the Territory because many weapons are registered with us by servicemen," he added.

Four years ago, the Territorial Legislature did away with the requirement of registering rifles and shotguns; all other firearms must be registered, however.

No one in the Territory can purchase a small arm without first acquiring a permit from the police departments of the various counties.

(Courtesy Honolulu Star Advertiser *Archives.)*

stadium! He had recorded background crowd noise and tapped a box with a pencil to simulate a hit. A really remarkable talent! This was done to offset the time difference for an expensive live transmission from California.

I realized that since I was no longer considering a Communications career, all this additional radio experience would not be particularly useful, but it was the best paying, most fun job, and easiest to get for the Christmas holidays.

When I was romancing with Shirley, I shared my success as a first-semester pre-med. She was so happy, talked of our future family (twins Timmy and Tammy), and gave me a Christmas gift: a cute little figurine of a doctor, which inspired me at the time, and which I have always treasured.

Kidnap!

To my surprise my high school broadcast mentor and dearest friend Don Chamberlain got in touch with me before I returned to Chicago and said he needed help. Naturally, I would happily do anything for Don. He said his wife had become "violent and crazy," had recently fired a gun in their home, and he feared for the safety of his three young children. Don wanted to get them to safety on the mainland in the care of his parents.

My assignment was to purchase specified warm clothing, sized for the 18-month-old twin girls and two-month-old boy, which they would need at their Northern California winter destination. Don gave me the money and instructions to meet him at the airport terminal with all the clothing. He had purchased tickets for all, under assumed names. We met, they all boarded, and disappeared.

In a few days, Don's wife Joey was calling me at the radio station begging for information about Don and the children, which she described as *kidnapped*. I really didn't know just where they were, and was pledged to silence, so I lied that I hadn't seen Don since the previous summer dinner.

HAPPIER DAYS: 25 years following the kidnap, my son Matt and I visited Don and his family. Shown here L-R is his son, Don's lady friend, my pal Trudy, and his daughter Donielle.

XI

CHALLENGING SEMESTER

Spring '58

Back in the dorm, I was pleased to learn that Father Small had left and Father Montville, S.J., was the new dorm supervisor. This was the second semester of my new 30 science hour pre-med program, and I buckled down to do the best job I could with that heavy load of day and night classes.

Side Jobs

One of my classmates, Bill Plante, learned of my experience in broadcasting and told me of a weekend job available at WNMP radio station in nearby Evanston, where he also had a part-time job. What a treat!

I applied for the job and was soon seated for the usual audition-reading. I remember the audition because I was handed a page of several paragraphs containing musical terminology, with no chance to look it over, a so-called "cold read." I was familiar with most of the terms, but blew it on one of the many listed: a word I had never seen before. I pronounced it *conTRAPuntal*, but later learned it is pronounced *contraPUNtal*. I got the job, but have never had the chance to properly pronounce the word since!

I was soon taking the train to Evanston early every Sunday morning, to open the station at 8am and lead a religious music and news program, hosting a couple of ministers' live sermon broadcasts until noon. It felt good to be back in radio, even for a few hours a week, and to make a few extra dollars.

Bill Plante went on to a career in broadcasting, and for decades I enjoyed hearing his news reports from the Capitol, the White House, and around the world for CBS.

Another Job?

Soon, a sign appeared on the dorm bulletin board, "Babysitter Wanted". I followed up and the job was occasional Saturday nights only, in an apartment building just a short walk from the dorm. Mr. and Mrs. Coyne would go downtown to the Chicago Loop for Saturday night dinner and entertainment, and I was to sit for baby Timothy.

He was in bed when I arrived and usually slept soundly all evening, so I could bring my books and have a quieter Saturday evening than I'd likely have in the dorm.

The dorm cafeteria was closed on weekends and these part-time jobs provided cash to cover necessities or my weekend meal. And the occasional beer.

I could handle these jobs because the radio was Sunday mornings only, and the babysitting was occasional Saturday nights. But with my heavy class schedule I didn't know if I'd have time for Dr. Jaskowski's lab job, but I wanted to learn more parasitology, so I quit the few hours a week that I was still working at Broadway Lincoln-Mercury, in favor of working with roundworms and rats. The now-infamous new Edsels were not selling well, and I got the feeling they might soon be discontinued. They were, the following year.

Rats and Worms

My lab job paid a little better than car washing, and I could set my own hours. First, I learned the life cycle of this roundworm. The *Ascaris* eggs were shed in pigs' feces and consumed by other pigs. Somewhere in the intestine these eggs hatched as tiny worms which burrowed through the intestinal wall and were carried by the blood stream to the lungs of the pig. There they developed in the alveoli, wriggled up into the bronchial tubes, were coughed up in mucus, and swallowed. They grew into adult worms, lived in the large intestine, shedding thousands of eggs into the feces, to infect other pigs and start the cycle over.

Ascaris: Dr. Jaskowski brought thousands of these fresh from the stockyards.

Sometimes the worms so filled the pig's large intestine that it became completely blocked, leading to the pig's sickness or death. Sick and dying pigs created a tremendous economic problem for the pork industry, and Dr. Jaskowski was seeking some way to break the life cycle, in order to halt the spread of the disease.

My assignment was first to maintain our healthy colony of white lab rats, which would be our test subjects. Dr. Jaskowski regularly visited the stock yards to collect the worms, returning to the lab with large Thermos jugs filled with wiggly worms for me to collect their eggs and infect my rats. I was looking for a factor in the rats' intestine that caused these eggs to hatch, so we might learn how to block that "hatching factor." I enjoyed the work, loved doing surgery on my anesthetized rats, and was bitten only once. We had strict practices regarding gloves, frequent hand washing and avoiding face-touching, lest I ingest some of the invisible eggs I was working with, thus infecting myself with my own intestinal worms.

Big "Date"

Since I was one of the few students who stayed in the dorm over the weekend, Father Montville, the new Director of the dorm, asked me to take his niece to an upcoming Saturday night party. He would provide a car and pay me $20 to escort her to the event her friends were hosting. I accepted the offer, later drove her to the forgettable event, made small-talk with strangers for hours, and afterward returned her and the car to her uncle at the dorm. She thanked me and disappeared, never to be seen again. I remember this only because it was my only actual *date* in my three years of college life in Chicago. Today I'd be labeled a "studious nerd," but I was chasing bigger dreams, and my social life was in Honolulu.

Big Thrill!

Early in the spring I received word from The Experiment in International Living (EIL) that I had been accepted for the homestay to Germany in the coming summer. In addition, a letter of recommendation from someone in Honolulu cited my high school speaking and writing activities, which earned me a $500 scholarship, as someone who could write or speak about my experience. *Providence?*

Our group leader would be Dr. Max Putzel, Professor of Philosophy and German Literature at Yale. Our group of ten Experimenters would assemble in New York and sail on the Holland-American *SS Rotterdam*. I spent part of the spring excitedly organizing and packing for the summer abroad. My parents sent me some souvenir Hawaiian gifts for my homestay family.

One of the instructive travel recommendations that I most remember was that after we had packed our bags, we were to "carry them twice around the block." This distance was twice four blocks, or just about a Chicago eight-block mile, after which we should return and "lighten our bags". Once around the block was enough for me; I got the message! This was to illustrate that there would be many walks from train station to hotel, or pier to train, and these were the days before wheeled luggage. (I've always wondered why it took so long for these to appear!)

I finished up the semester with very satisfactory grades, despite long lab courses, night chemistry class, and working in the worm lab. I arranged to take a summer break from rat-worm lab, radio, and babysitting, and before I knew it, was on the train to New York.

XII

My Experiment

Summer '58

Our group of ten met with Dr. Putzel and his wife Nell, enjoyed an orientation dinner and the following morning we boarded our ship for Europe. "Dr. Max" told us he had fled Germany with other Jews in 1939, and this was his first return. Our group was a very pleasant collection of guys and girls, all collegians with various majors.

My Experiment

Our ship's passengers, aboard the Holland-American *SS Rotterdam*, were exclusively college kids. Some were other Experimenters going to different countries, others were students heading to various European summer school programs. The voyage lasted about a week. We met with Dr. Putzel (now "Max") every morning, where he described the EIL philosophy, the summer program, our homestays, various expectations and responsibilities, along with some German language and cultural lessons.

It had been only a little over a decade since Germany's utter devastation in World War II. The Russian Communists had seized the Eastern half of the country, as well as half of Berlin, the capital. We would be living around Bonn, at that time the Provisional Capital of free West Germany, on the Rhine south of Cologne (Koeln). Our local leader would be a graduate student, Fritz Hohrmann, who had recruited the ten brave families that would each accept an American college kid for six weeks homestay.

Evenings aboard the ship were fabulous collegiate social events, dancing, flirting, and partying. I don't think I had ever been surrounded by so many girls since elementary school! On this Dutch ship, the drink of choice was Heineken Beer. Most of us were not familiar with Heineken and were initially unaware that it was stronger than American beer. Guzzling incautiously could lead to surprisingly sudden intoxication.

Brother Bob: Spring '58 my brother Bob in his Punahou ROTC uniform, soon to graduate.

Ouch!

One night, full of beer and gaily galloping down a passageway, I leaped over the lower sill of those "flood doors" – forgetting the overhead portion – and slammed my forehead into the *upper* sill! I was briefly dazed, but did not lose consciousness; nevertheless, the ship's doc decided that I might have suffered a concussion, so prescribed the standard treatment of three days flat in bed. It was quite boring, and I missed the partying fun, though I appreciated the daily *bed bath* by a charming Dutch nurse.

About Jews

Max visited me daily and once brought me a bottle of *711 Cologne* (from Cologne), "For your *morale*." I was so impressed by Max's kindness and empathy for my bedridden situation. I recalled my dad's words when I asked him, when I was about ten years old, "What is it about Jews? I hear different things about them."

Dad said, "John, Jews are among the finest people you will ever meet: honest, smart, sincere, hard-working and loyal friends. Some of them are stereotyped as being unpleasantly greedy, but I've met very few." I remembered my '56 girlfriend Alice, and her very sweet Jewish family and friends.

On these visits Max caught me up on the summer program: We would live for six weeks in our German homes where there would be one or more young persons of about our age, our German "brother or sister." At least one person would speak *some* English. After homestay, our group would travel for two weeks by bus with our German companions to major cities and sites in West Germany. This tour would be followed by a week of free travel before heading home. It all sounded so exciting!

After my release from the sickbay, I was able to enjoy a few final days of the partying before arrival. Upon landing in Rotterdam, as promised, we walked uphill to the train station, grateful for the sage advice to lighten our bags back home. We took the train to Bonn where we met with our local leader, Fritz, who gave each of us the information and locations for our new homes and briefed us on our adopted families.

Once on German soil, we wondered if the return might be pretty uncomfortable for Max, who had fled the *Gestapo* (German Secret Police) 19 years ago. But his only comment I heard was, "The police still have the same-style hats!"

Oberkassel

I was assigned to the village of Oberkassel and the home of Herr Dr. Heinz Friedrich Schulz, a member of the Finance Ministry, his wife Paula, and their two children, Ingebord ("Inge"), 19, who worked in a textile factory, and Wilfried, 17, a *gymnasium* (high school) student. I roomed with Wilfried, and we got along just fine, since there were only two years between us. Everyone in the family spoke some English, and they all wanted to learn more. My German was certainly adequate, but I was woefully lacking in vocabulary.

Homestay

My life with the Schulzes was delightful. I enjoyed all the unique meals Frau Schulz prepared and noticed they didn't have as much meat as we would. All meals were accompanied by German white wine, a single glass for us minors.

Biking

Inge loaned me her bicycle, and I loved biking to town on errands for Frau Schulz. She gave me daily shopping or errand lists to practice my Deutsch with each of the merchants: grocer, butcher, baker, post office, etc. (No supermarket then.) I was delighted to go to each of these locations to place my order in German from my list. These daily encounters helped rapidly to expand my vocabulary.

After my morning errand runs, Frau Schulz and I had lunch together, usually cold cuts, since Dr. Schulz and Inge were at work and Wilfred was at school. In the afternoons I enjoyed riding to the nearby *Siebengeberge* (Seven Dwarfs) mountains and the picturesque town of *Koenigswinter*; several times I climbed to the hilltop ruins of the 11th Century *Drachenfels* (Dragon Rock) castle, where I made a great painting of the romantic ruins. (Wish I could find it!)

Big Questions

When I discretely asked Dr. Schulz about the Nazi slaughter of millions of Jews, he responded, "John, dear John, we just *had no idea* that was happening! We knew Jews were taken from the major cities, but were told they were simply being re-located to the East countryside. We had *no idea*! Es war Unglaublich! (It was unbelievable!)"

I was also interested in his description of the Nazi desperation as the Allied armies crossed the Rhine and rolled in. Along with other office workers, he was given a rifle and sent to "guard the *Autobahn* (freeway)," along with *Hitler-Jugen* (Hitler-Youth), conscripted 10-14 year olds in uniform. "Imagine," he said, "rifles against tanks! *Furchtar!* (dreadful!)" He seemed very sincere and truthful.

Bierstube

I loved biking country roads into forests where it seemed there was a German tavern (*Bier Stube*) every few miles. I enjoyed hours of riding in the woods, along with lots of good German beer. As a slightly tan stranger in a tavern, I was an object of polite, curious conversation, which I enoyed. This was the first time a bartender had offered me "*Bier mit Ei?*" ("An egg in your beer?") Not bad at all!

Cultural Weekends

Each weekend Dr. Schulz took Frau Shultz, Wilfried, and me in their Volkswagen Bug down the Rhine to visit various castles and vineyards. He taught us about different Rhine wine varietals and purchased several bottles for the coming week. We visited so many medieval villages, castles and historical monuments, that each weekend drive was a valuable cultural experience. I became fascinated by German castles along the Rhine, especially their towers (*Tuerme*), and 62 years later, I finally built a tower of my own, at my home on Molokai!

Group Socials

Each Saturday evening our group of ten Experimenters and ten German brothers or sisters gathered at a local tavern for socializing. We danced, ate and drank, and had fun, but the part I most remember was the eagerness and the thrill of *speaking English* to our fellow Americans! It's difficult to explain the feeling, but we had hardly spoken a word of conversational English for the past week, and when we did speak, it ... was ... always ... carefully ... enunciated ... and ... slowly ... delivered ... in ... correct ... phrases ... so ... that ... our ... words ... could ... be ... understood ... by ... our ... German ... family ... and ... friends.

Now we were overjoyed by the opportunity to "jabberrapidlyincolloquialslang-filled English!" One of the girls, Babs Roberts, expressed the feeling so well, when she said, "I just get so horny to jabber slang in English, you know?"

Herr Dr. und Frau H. F. Schulz, taken several years later.

I built my very own tower on Molokai, placing every block by hand, in 2000.

Touring

Our homestays seemed to pass so quickly, and soon all twenty of us brothers and sisters joined Max, Fritz, and Nell to tour the German countryside in our bus. We enjoyed the lectures, museums, and city tours by day, but even more fun were our nightly accommodations in *youth hostels* (*Jugendherberge*). Some hostels were in barns on farms, others in school gyms, or even castles, and we shared them with other groups of young people hiking or cycling across the country, chattering in half a dozen languages. The hostels were "minimalistic": plain meals, cold showers, hard beds, crowded dorms smelling of sweaty cyclists or hikers, but there was something colorful and fun, feeling like being part of an international community, in these youthful dormitories.

Bonding

On the tour, ten Germans and our ten Americans completely blended into twenty brothers and sisters in one happy family. This certainly was the intent of The Experiment. There were strong friendships and even mini-romances within our group. I enjoyed quite a cuddly "crush" on lovely Renata, but when I pressed for a little more intimacy, she sweetly replied, "*Dass ist nur fuer mein Mann.*" (*That* is only for my [future] husband.)

Lifelong friendships developed between most Experimenters and their new families. Personally, I've remained closely connected with my Schulz family for over sixty years and have friendly relations with the children and even grandchildren of my German brother and sister. I know Doctor and Frau Schulz would be so pleased!

My sister Sally was so inspired by my stories that she went to Japan on the Experiment six years later in 1964 and found it equally as educational and enjoyable. She even climbed Mt.Fuji! Sally later returned to teach English in Japan.

XIII

THE PARTY'S OVER

Wise Refusal

During the tour, John Mason, one of our group, sought Max Putzel's approval for him to remain in Germany for an academic year. John was a political science major and would enroll in the University of Bonn. I thought it would be just wonderful to have a year to cruise the Rhine, bike through the forests, and seek a sweet young *fraulein* to help improve my *Deutsch*. Max approved of John's plan, but refused to let me stay: "Right in the middle of your compressed pre-med program, if you get off the track for a year, John, you may never get back on track. I know it would be fun, but if you can get into med school after just three college years, you've saved yourself a year and can return to pay yourself back *after* your MD." He certainly was right, and I'm grateful for Max's good advice and my academic success. But I'm still trying to recapture that pay-back year in Germany! *Thanks, Max!*

Phil and Kaki

I made a very good friend in our Experiment crew. Phil Miller of Middlebury College in Vermont, whose family lived in Chicago, suggested it would be great fun to get together in Chicago for beers the following semester. My other close pal was "Kaki" (Katherine) Rupkey from Mt. Holyoke in Massachusetts. Kaki and I decided to travel together for the coming free travel week.

Final Celebration

After our tour, our group re-joined our families for a final dinner celebrating the magnificent two months we had all spent together. There were so many tearful farewells! Our Experiment taught us so much about ourselves and our German families, as well as their language and their great culture. I think we all agreed this was an *immensely valuable* summer adventure, and likely one of the most unforgettable experiences of our lives. It has certainly been one for me! And to think this magnificent adventure began with that *stranger on a train* a year ago. Sure seems like *Providence* to me!

Memorable Banner

Great Experiment souvenir.

Before I left for the free travel week, my German sister Inge presented me with a marvelous gift: at her textile factory, she chose a cloth on which to sew more than one hundred of the Stoffabzeichen (municipal and souvenir patches), that I had collected from all the places I visited. What a labor of love! Nearly 3x5 feet, she created a beautiful memory-banner, which hangs proudly in my stairwell!

Free Travel

Kaki and I partnered for this free week. We first stopped in Belgium for *Expo '58*, the Brussels' World's Fair, the first of its kind since before World War II. We left with souvenir *Atomiums*, the symbol of the Expo.

Our next stop was London, and what I most remember was that, viewing English people in the streets, Kaki said, "If they didn't speak English, we would think this is a second-rate city!"

Bidet story

Then to Paris for the *Tour Eiffel*, *Arc de Triumph*, *Louvre* and other great attractions. We spent a couple of nights in a cheap hotel which had a wash basin and *bidet* in the room, but toilets and showers were in a bathroom at the end of the hall. Kaki was impressed by the "cute little foot bath."

This was my first experience with a *bidet*, a truly invaluable appliance. Kaki was not wrong, it can be used as a foot bath, but for the practical and romantic French, it was primarily a *bottom bath*, to freshen your private or amorous parts. Great for adult daily hygiene.

Reflection

Since then, I've installed a *bidet* in every home I've owned, including our motorhome! They are great for babies' bottoms between diaper changes. Great for adult bottoms, as well, and save a lot of toilet paper. Today, my *bidet* is what I most miss when traveling. You can now buy an advanced Bidet: all the usual washing functions, plus warm-air "blow dry," contained in a novel toilet seat: Toto. But I favor the simple, efficient, original design.

Here's my original Kohler bidet.

Kaki and I were both *controlling* personalities. I complained that she was *crabby*, and she grumbled that I was *cranky*. During our week together, as well as in subsequent correspondence, we addressed each other as "crank" and "crab."

Happy Birthday!

Then back to Rotterdam for our sail home, where I finally got the chance to lose my virginity: a twentieth birthday gift to myself. Before leaving Germany, I had received a birthday card and cash from my dad. I went down to the sailor bars and brothels near the wharf. The "ladies" sat behind big picture windows in apartment rows, "come hither" gesturing, and counting with their fingers to negotiate prices with sidewalk potential customers. I had a couple of drinks for calming, negotiated a price with one of the women, nervously stepped up to her door, and entered.

Although the picture window was six feet wide, the "room" wasn't much longer and barely four feet deep. The mattress on the floor was dirty, and the prostitute was as unpleasant as the degrading experience. But finally the job was done. It was over at long last! Happy birthday, baby!

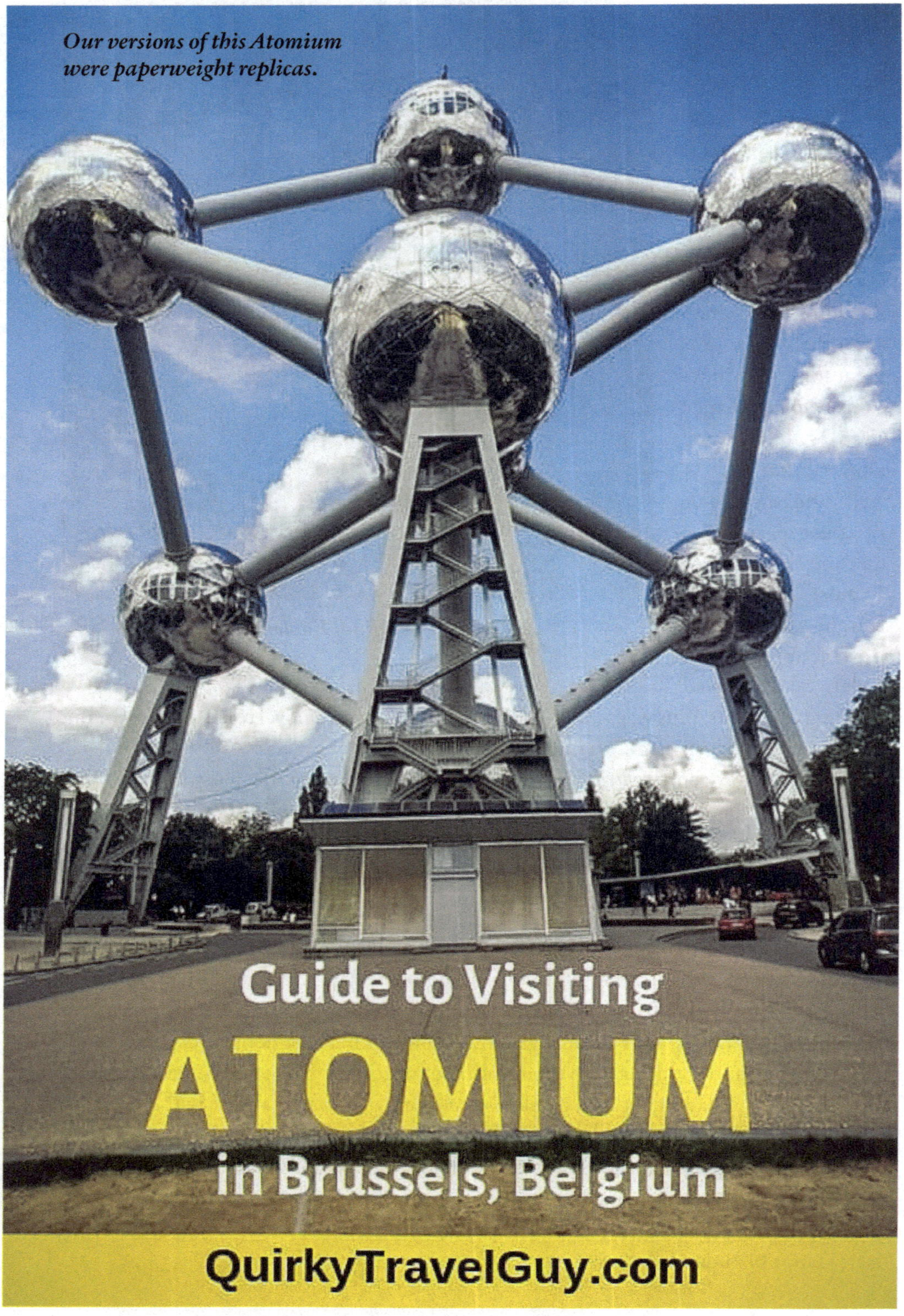

Our versions of this Atomium were paperweight replicas.

XIV

FINAL PRE-MED PREP YEAR

Fall '58

Back in the dorm in late August, I began my final year of cramming science courses. In order to assure that my GPA would qualify for medical school admission, I persuaded my dad to contribute the extra cost of a private room, since I'd be carrying my heaviest course load yet. He generously agreed, and I moved alone into a nice room at the quiet end of the hallway, overlooking Sheridan Road. Having no roommate allowed me to set up an unusual and rigorous study routine. After dinner I would sleep in the evening, arising at midnight to study uninterrupted during the wee hours of the night.

Applications

After resuming fall classes, my first priority was those medical school applications. I started with my favorite, the University of Illinois College of Medicine at the Chicago Westside Medical Center. Then the Loyola University Medical School, also in Chicago, and finally, at the urging of Max Putzel, I also applied to Yale Med School. Max wrote me a glowing letter of endorsement for Yale, which I copied and attached to my other two applications as well. Each of these applications required fees and several hours of forms, provision of transcripts, MCAT scores, letters of recommendation, a questionnaire, and an essay.

MCAT

The next step was the grueling Medical College Aptitude Test (MCAT) in November. This was a handwritten and multiple-choice, proctored exam which I believe was given in two parts, lasting all day. It seemed to cover broad general knowledge: a bit of everything I ever learned on any subject! We never saw our scores, which were sent directly to the schools to which we'd applied.

Decisions

Acceptance decisions would not be made until the following semester after midterms in our final required courses. We were approaching the total number of science hours needed to qualify. At this point there was nothing to do but study hard, get great grades, and wait.

Loyola's pre-med program was highly regarded for the preparedness of its graduates, so I felt I had a good chance for med school admission, despite my compressed curriculum. The courses were strict, competition was harsh, and the Loyola dropout rate – between freshman entry and med school application – was said to be at least 50%. There are many explanations why students quit.

Expectations of Med School Applicants

There seemed to be, for example, an unspoken feeling in the pre-med program that physicians should be tough: strong enough to handle whatever stresses might be thrown their way in terms of future blood and gore, patients' physical and emotional distress, various physical challenges, etc. Physicians were expected to be strong and resilient, to show *equanimity* and grace under pressure. There was a war on, and most young physicians would be immediately drafted to serve the military.

For these reasons, I suppose the training was intended to be *stressful*, to see which students might simply cave under pressure, drop out, and choose a more suitable career path. Better to drop out now than in med school, where there'd be many more stressful situations. One of several Loyola purposeful stressors was the dissection course of Dr. Boris Spiroff.

Stress Tests

Dr. Spiroff's biology class included dissection of the earthworm, which was intended to be a purposely difficult dissection of some sixty tiny parts. Each student was provided an earthworm on a wax dissection tray (A 6 x 12 metal tray, containing about half an inch of firm wax for insertion of specimen pins), and was instructed to return in a week to demonstrate his dissection. Manual skills were tested by our ability to perform a particularly careful dissection of those tiny earthworm parts and memorize their names, so we could identify and recite them for Dr. Spiroff.

On the day of my exam, I was called into the darkened test lab, nervously holding my dissection tray. I placed it on the table before Spiroff, under a single suspended spotlight. He directed me to use my long, fine pointer to touch and recite each of the sixty memorized parts from front to rear, within three minutes.

With my pointer trembling a little, Spiroff started the loud clock: *Tick-tock! Tick-tock!* As fast as I could, I began touching and reciting each of the tiny parts in order, while he watched closely. *Tick-tock! Tick-tock!* When I missed one, he interrupted me, saying, "Show me that again."

This pause lost precious seconds and made me momentarily forget my place in the recitation. I became even more nervous, racing against the loud *Tick-tock! Tick-tock!*, as fast as I could! But not too fast – or I'd miss one – and I'd be interrupted again. *Tick-tock! Tick-tock!* Rushing or trembling would cause errors and lost time! *Tick-tock! Tick-tock!*

It was a really stressful race against the clock, and maintaining self-control was critical. Suddenly there was a loud *Bang!* of the timer, and the race was over! I had correctly identified almost all of the parts and was dripping in sweat! Spiroff recorded a grade in his notebook, thanked me, and I was out the door.

It was certainly a relief! I had heard stories of some students who had completely lost control of themselves. They had trembled so much that they couldn't use their pointer, failed the recitation, and completely blew their exam. Some left the room in tears, or crazily muttering worm parts to themselves, while wildly stabbing their pointers in the air! Ouch! Some of these students soon changed their majors.

There were plenty of other stressors, such as frequent surprise organic chemistry recitations: "Now Mr. Corboy, name nine amino acids." Or, "Corboy, describe the molecular structure of six carbohydrates."

Most difficult for me were Organic Chemistry synthesis exams. As an example, the student was provided a description of one or two molecules at the top of the test page with the instruction, "With *this*, Make *this*:, (another molecule or compound)". On the page one needed to demonstrate the chain of equations demonstrating the reactions needed to produce the expected product at the bottom. It usually required at least half a dozen reactions; there was no way to prepare or cheat.

In physics, we learned to work rapidly with our *slide rules*, ingenious devices which I'd never used before. (These were the days long before pocket calculators.)

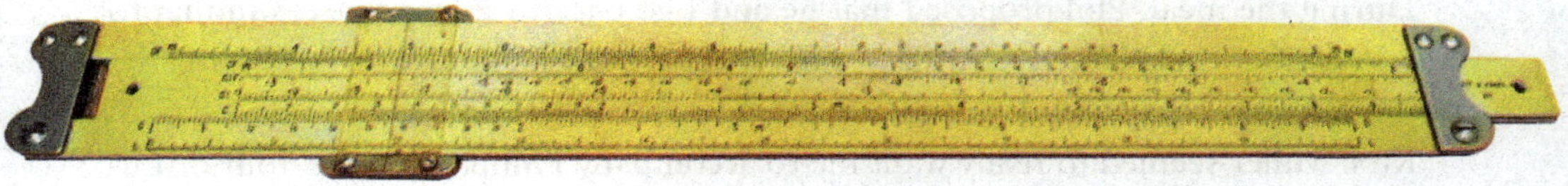

Remarkably accurate, these vanished when digital calculators arrived

Strenuous Schedule

To really take control of my study hours, I cut back on my afternoon and weekend work with rats and worms, to make room for lab courses. I dropped the babysitting but kept the Sunday morning WNMP radio job, just for a brief change of scene. I set up a rigorous schedule to maximize my study time. At 6:00pm I would socialize with my friends over dinner. By 7:00pm was in bed. I slept 'til midnight, got up and made instant coffee with my little electric cup-coil, and turned on "Music Til Dawn" with Jay Andres. Sponsored by American Airlines, this all-night classical music program provided an entertaining musical education: Jay described each piece, composer, orchestra, and perhaps some history. A terrific accompaniment to histology, embryology, and organic chemistry. With the music, No-Doze (caffeine) pills, and coffee, I worked 'til

6am, showered, and met friends for breakfast at 7. Classes were 8 until 3 – or 5 with labs – then dinner at 6 with the boys, to start the cycle over again. It was always easy to fall asleep at 7. But sleeping at odd hours was good conditioning for future med school "on call" schedules.

Weekend Nutrition

The dorm cafeteria was closed on weekends, and I resumed my previously-described weird weekend meal plan of stale donuts, old fruit, and Sunday's fried chicken-liver feast.

Thanksgiving Adventure Plan

Phil Miller flew in from school in Vermont for the long Thanksgiving weekend and invited me to his home for the traditional meal. His parents were older, formal, and quite elegant. His mother was a grand-daughter of George M. Pullman, developer of the famed Pullman Railroad Sleeping Car, and her family was "old money" wealthy. Phil's dad was Professor of Medicine at the University of Chicago Med School. They frequented the opera and symphony and traveled widely.

They kept two servants at home. European ladies, I believe; one of whom was the cook. I recall the meal particularly, because Mrs. Miller had a push-button under the table beneath her foot, which she used to summon a servant. When the soup was served, I promptly picked up the salt shaker – whereupon she crossly corrected me, saying, "John, stop! To season before tasting is a serious insult to the cook. *Never do that*!" Ouch! So I have never done so since.

During the meal, Phil proposed that he and I go back to Europe next summer to travel together. I explained that this would be nice, but I planned to work during the summer to cover expenses of my hoped-for admission to medical school next fall.

Mrs. Miller seemed to really want me to accompany Philip on a boys' tour of Europe: I think she felt he was a little too "straightlaced" and formal, and that I was perhaps an adventuresome, but safe, companion that might help him to loosen up a bit. She offered the Pullman Foundation to pay my year's educational expenses so that I would not need to work for the summer and could accompany Philip. Quite a tempting proposal!

Christmas '58

Europe next summer with Phil sounded like fun, so I gratefully accepted. During the rest of the academic year, Phil and I worked out the plan. We met again when he returned to Chicago for Christmas vacation; this was the first Christmas I did not go home.

My parents were understandably disappointed, but Shirley's family was being transferred, so I'd miss romancing with her. I wanted to wrap up my work with the rats and worms, do some extra reading, visit my grandmother, and just relax for a couple weeks. Phil and I enjoyed crafting trip plans over frosty mugs of imported draft Czech *Pilsener*

Urquel, his expensive favorite brew, at a Chicago Loop bar.

My grades arrived, and I was pleased to see that I had done quite well. It was clear that my current compulsive study schedule was proving successful. By sleeping all evening, I avoided the constant interruptions typical of dorm life, and by studying after midnight, I essentially avoided all casual distractions and could concentrate.

I had pleasant Christmas visits with my Grandma Lavinia and dad's old friend, attorney Bill Burns. I loved going to dinner at Bill and his sisters' apartment, because he always slipped me a $20 bill, which was a big treat!

Long Distance

Although my thrifty parents always said, "Write, don't call," I decided to call my parents at Christmas. We weren't allowed to use the dorm telephone for *long distance* calls, so I had to use the sidewalk *phone booth* across the street.

One of 2.6 million pay phones, now extinct!

HISTORICAL NOTE

Payphone History: The first payphones were invented in 1901, and evolved through many improvements and cabinets (phone booths) to be placed on many city streets in the 1920s. By 1960, Bell Telephone celebrated 1 million pay phones, and by the peak in 1995, there were 2.6 million payphones, with one on almost every U.S. city street corner.

The first cell phones arrived in '83, costing $4000. As price and size have fallen, the market has exploded, and the payphone has become obsolete; between 2001 and 2011, payphone companies all closed service down, and their payphones and phone booths disappeared.

My grandchildren have never seen one of these ubiquitous side-walk conveniences, even used by Superman!

Payphone

To use the *payphone*, I arrived with a pocket full of quarters, dropped in a dime to reach the *operator*, and gave her the number I wanted to call. She then told me how many quarters to drop in the slot. (*Long-distance* charges were higher weekdays, lower evenings and weekends.) Each dropped quarter rang a bell for the operator to hear and count the total coins. Once the charge had been deposited, usually between *sixteen and twenty dings* for a three-minute, *long-distance* call, she then connected me with my parents.

HISTORICAL NOTE

Radio-telephone: Because trans-Pacific calls were transmitted by radio across the ocean (so-called "radio-telephone"), there was a slight transmission delay because the radio signals was reflected off the stratosphere. If the called party responded too quickly, or interrupted, it would block the incoming signal. If both parties spoke at once, the signal was blocked *both* ways. To slow down radio-telephone conversations and avoid confusion, parties were to indicate the end of their statement by saying, "Over." This told the other party to begin. So for example, I said, "Hi, everybody! How's Christmas at your house? Over." Then they would reply in the same way, "... Over." The radio-telephone service was replaced by the undersea Trans-Pacific coaxial fiberoptic cable in 1964.

It seems so strange today, when terms like *phonebooth*, *payphone*, *operator*, and *long-distance* sound like foreign words, and most young people have never seen a phone booth or payphone; but that's how we made calls in the '40s, '50s, and early '60s. Yet we thought this convenient long-distance service was the height of modern technology. And it was, then.

Life Within

Since I was committed to medicine, even if I didn't get accepted this coming year, I thought I would buy myself a microscope. I found an antique one in a pawn shop: a monocular *Ernst Leitz* from Germany, which I gave myself for Christmas. It was fun looking at microscopic things such as the invisible worm eggs. I pricked a finger and studied the red blood corpuscles. One day I got the bright idea to examine my semen to see if there really were *sperm cells*. Wow, it was amazing to see those thousands of microscopic swimmers, zooming this way and that, wiggling their little tails, seeking an egg to fertilize! This was actual *life inside me!* Imagine this kind of *life* – within my ejaculate! Risky stuff!

XV

Final Semester

Spring '59

Once classes began, I buckled down to what I hoped would be my last college semester. I became a virtual hermit on my crazy schedule, but it was really working for me: grinding through the night with caffeine and "Music Til Dawn".

Heart-Lung Machine

One evening at dinner, my only social time, Allen was talking about new developments in cardiology: specifically, *heart-lung machines*. These could *mechanically* replace circulation and respiration, allowing *open-heart surgery*. He suggested we might think of creating an animal heart-lung machine project for the upcoming spring Loyola Science Fair. This sounded like a worthwhile and fun project, and in succeeding dinners we discussed the idea. My rats were too small, and I had been doing some experimental guinea pig surgery in my room on weekends, but these were not much larger.

We decided a rabbit would be best. I called a local pharmaceutical company and asked about a donation of some lab rabbits. I represented that we were "researchers in a lab at Loyola University" (mostly true), so they offered us a large package of feed and half a dozen lovely white rabbits that had been used for evaluation of some eye drops, but otherwise were normal and healthy. I kept them alongside my rats in my worm lab at school.

Over the coming weekends we designed a heart-lung machine. I had experience working with Erector Set motors and parts in grade school, and Allen got IV (intravenous) tubing and syringes from his father Dr. Edward Zencka. We got a small oxygen tank, along with anti-frothing and anticoagulant agents through his father.

I got a bag of outdated human blood from the Blood Bank, to test our system. The blood was contained in an IV bottle, into which we bubbled oxygen from our tank. The Erector Set motor moved syringes back and forth to pump the blood forward toward a simulated "rabbit," then back to the reservoir IV bottle. The anti-coagulants and anti-frothing chemicals proved essential.

I had a can of ether from my guinea pig surgery, so on later weekends we did some practice surgery and machine testing with rabbits and their blood, and it seemed to work well. Allen's dad gave us a couple of white lab coats to look the part, so by the spring we were ready for the Science Fair.

The ether kept the rabbit asleep while we connected inflow to his aorta, outflow from the vena cava, completely bypassing his heart for an *hour.* We won *First Prize*, which I'm sure looked good on our resumes! *Thanks, Allen and Dr. Zencka!*

Thrilling Letter

Early in the year, I received a letter from the University of Illinois College of Medicine, inviting me to a personal interview! This was a very good sign and I excitedly responded. On the appointed day I put on my suit, took the train to the West Side Medical Center and nervously climbed the stone steps of the huge gray Gothic buildings.

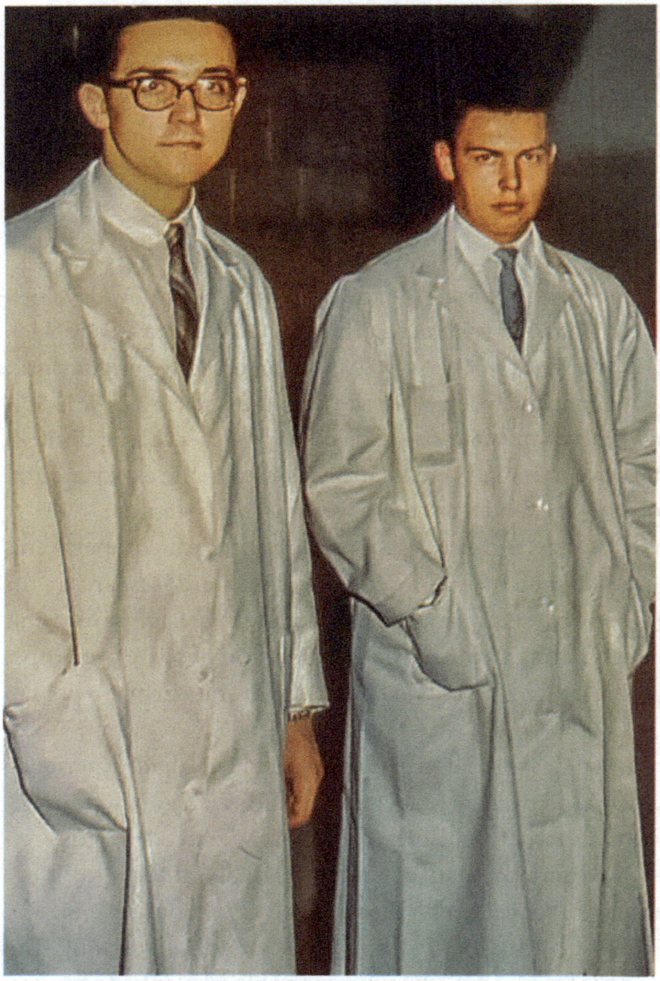

Allen and me in our "researcher" costumes.

The interview went smoothly. My physician-interviewer was pleasant, encouraging me to describe my family, education, health, background, and especially my motivation. There were the expected questions about future plans and my reasons for wanting to become a physician. It helped to explain my motivation when I reported that my father was a doctor, and I was familiar with his joy in caring for his patients.

I was told that acceptance would depend on the results of my midterm exams this semester. Yippee! I remember that I danced joyfully back to the train station for the ride home! I felt

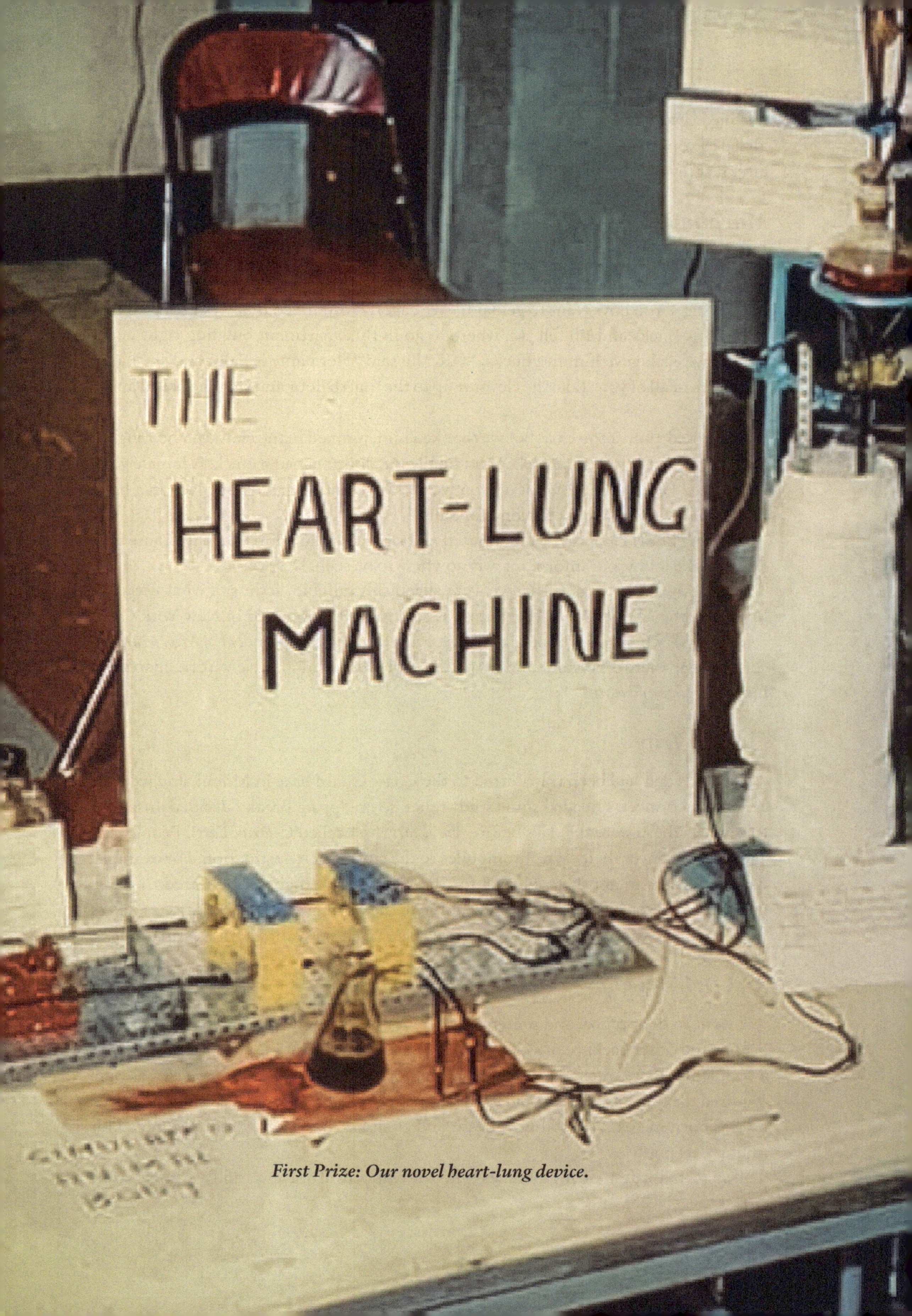

First Prize: Our novel heart-lung device.

quite confident about my being accepted. Later, Loyola Med School accepted me, Yale declined. The details are a bit blurry now, but I recall the joyous tide of emotion as I realized the opportunity to fulfill my dream of a medical career was ever more likely. And after just my two *grueling* years of pre-med!

Murphy Man

One weekend night several of us guys were out ambling aimlessly through a nearby neighborhood of apartment buildings when we were approached by a swarthy older guy asking, "You boys want to get laid?" We eagerly responded that we sure did. "Give me twenty bucks and I'll tell you where to go in this apartment building right here." I think we each gave him five bucks. "OK," he said "Her name is Sally, and she'll take good care of all of you. Take the elevator up to the fourth floor and ring the bell at apartment 410."

It seemed almost too easy, but we thanked him, jumped in the elevator and rang the bell at 410. There was some delay, and finally the door opened a crack. A female voice called out, "Who's there? What do you want?" We could see an elderly lady in a bathrobe. Charlie said, "We are looking for Sally."

"Wrong door! Go away!" She shouted and slammed the door. When we came back down to the lobby, our informant was nowhere to be seen.

It quickly dawned on us that we were sheepishly gullible victims of what was once known as the *Murphy Man*. The scam was said to have originated in New York City a century ago, when horny fools like us were directed to "*the apartment of Mrs. Murphy*," certain that there'd be someone named Murphy listed in any New York apartment building. *Live and learn!*

Florida Trip

Shirley's dad had been transferred to the Coast Guard base in Miami, and we were eager to reconnect. I needed some study relief, so on Spring Break I decided on a drive to Miami. These were the days before *rental cars* (first called *U-Drive Cars*). People paid agencies to deliver their own automobiles to the city of their destination. For example, Midwesterners might fly to Florida for the winter, have their car delivered to them, then returned to them after they flew home in the Spring. *AAA Driveaway* was one of the bigger firms and they aggressively advertised "Drivers Wanted, All Destinations."

AAA Driveaway

I went to their office, and pretended to be John D. Kloppenburg with "his" driver's license and other backup cards. For a Social Security number, I used my own with only a couple numbers transposed, so I wouldn't forget my fake SS number. Drivers were required to be at least 25 years old for insurance coverage. His driver's license indicated he was born in 1932, so he'd now be 26 and eligible. Not yet 21, I still resembled his military ID photo.

I collected a few of my buddies who all chipped in for gas, and we took turns driving to Miami. They disappeared to beaches on arrival. After I delivered the car, I spent several hot and humid, romantic days with Shirley and her family.

I arranged with AAA for a car to return to Chicago, when I learned that my friends had already found another way home. So I drove alone, straight through, 1400 miles, on coffee and No-Doze pills, except for a catnap at a Safeway parking lot. After almost 24 hours (no freeways then), I safely arrived at the owner's apartment near school, and received a five-dollar tip.

Reflection

Looking back, I realize how crazy that was to falsify my age – completely irresponsible – because an accident or injury would not be covered by insurance. But when we are young, we are foolishly confident that tragedies only happen to others.

Summer Prep

Back in Chicago, I met with Phil Miller before he returned to school, and we reviewed our plans for the coming summer's European adventure. His mom would arrange *contract cars* and *letters of credit* for us, and the Pullman Foundation was ready to send fall tuition money when requested.

I made sure my midterm exam results were forwarded to U of I Med School, and kept my fingers crossed.

Great News!

The big yellow U of I envelope arrived in May. My heart leapt at its *thickness*: a rejection notice would be a single page. Along with the glorious *Letter of Acceptance*, the packet was filled with information about the scholastic calendar, first-year curriculum, Student Residence Hall, tuition and fees, required books and supplies, fraternities, etc.

I could not have been more excited and immediately wrote to my parents. I'm sure they were pleased that I saved the year of room and board. But the big thrill for all of us was that Little Johnny Corboy was on his way to a degree in Medicine! This was the beginning of my career and new life as a *physician*, if – *if* - I could manage the impending four years of medical education. But I was pretty confident: if hard work was the key to success, I guessed I'd make it.

I'm heading to med school, Rob returning to college; with Sally, Mom, and Dad, August '59.

Part 2

Medical School

XVI

Return to Europe

Europe with Phil, '59

I gave my notice to the dorm to hold my mail and luggage, until I returned later in the summer. As soon as Phil and I were finished with classes, we met in New York and flew to London. There we met his parents who were attending an elegant reception celebrating the Nobel Prize Award of famed immunologist Sir Peter Medawar, and we attended a symphony concert with the Millers. Mrs. Miller had arranged *letters of credit* for us at selected banks along our intended routes. These would allow us to withdraw money as needed during our trip. (This was long before the days of universal credit cards.) She also arranged *contract cars* for our travels, since there was no such thing as a rental car.

We first drove the British Isles in our Austin: Scotland and Edinburgh, then England and London, staying in small hotels. Then we crossed the channel where another contract auto, a Volkswagen "Bug," awaited us in Cologne. We really enjoyed being in Germany once again and visiting last summer's Experiment pals; we also loved speaking the language. We stayed in *pensions* (bed and breakfasts) and enjoyed regular lunches on the road, feasting on long bread loaves, *wurst und Kaese* (sausage and cheese), along with beer or wine. Phil spoke better German than me, and I regularly learned new words and phrases from him. I recall one *pension* that I felt was too expensive for my budget, so I slept in the car (with mosquitoes) and missed breakfast. Poor decision!

We especially enjoyed staying in *Jugendherberge* (youth hostels), both for the economy and for the fun of the different languages and cultures. These hostels, in barns, school gyms, old castles, etc., were only for hikers or cyclists, not for automobile travelers. (Our Experiment bus group had been waivered.) We felt that although Mrs. Miller had provided us with an automobile, we were just as strapped for cash as these hikers and bikers. So we usually parked our VW a mile away from the hostel and hiked the distance with our backpacks. I remember that we were once unceremoniously evicted from a hostel that had discovered our car in the nearby woods and ejected us for breaking the rules.

Relieved Accomplishment

We finished our travels in Paris. After visiting all the famous sites, Phil, now 21, reported that it was high time he dropped his virginity. We located a so-called "red-light district," where he was accosted by a *hooker* on the street. He followed her up a narrow apartment stairwell and left me sitting at the bottom guarding the stairs, holding his ubiquitous camera and *Time* magazine. When he returned, I could see that his feeling of *relieved accomplishment* was much like mine had been the previous summer. What a relief to have *the task* over with! Curiously, just like my experience, his was not a pleasant one, but rather a grim but necessary rite of passage.

I couldn't help feeling that this was the kind of thing his mother was hoping would be part of his summer adventure with this "bad boy."

BMW

I had become a great fan of German engineering, typified by BMW (Bavarian Motor Works), and wanted some inexpensive, easy-to-park transportation around the med center. So before we left Paris, I purchased a BMW 250cc single-cylinder motorcycle and arranged to have it shipped to Allen Zencka's home in Chicago, since I had no idea where I'd be living.

Afterthoughts

As I flew back to Chicago, my thoughts were occupied with the challenge of the upcoming four years of medical school. Getting accepted, after three years of college (and really only *two* years of day and night science courses), was quite an accomplishment.

Yet I knew the real challenges lay ahead. Because of my crazy three-year curriculum, I wouldn't earn a degree from Loyola. Despite all the biological science, to qualify as a biology *major* I'd still need courses such as botany, along with additional liberal arts language and history courses to earn a B.S. Degree. Was I burning that bridge? If I flunk med school, could I come back to finish college and at least get a degree? I'd more likely be immediately drafted to serve in the burgeoning conflict in Vietnam.

There was still a short time before U of I classes would begin, and my parents wanted me to visit them in the interim, because it was uncertain when I'd be home again after med school began. So I made a quick trip, to enjoy a lovely reunion with my happy family. My dad told me how proud he was; I think he was even more excited than me! ***Big challenges ahead!***

XVII

Moving In

Fall '59: Fraternities

Back in Chicago, as I reviewed my summer mail in the dorm, there were several letters from medical fraternities inviting me to visit them during the upcoming Rush Week. This was described as four evenings, visiting each of the four National Medical Fraternities. They were recruiting freshmen to join their fraternity and consider living in their frat house. These were all located along Ashland Avenue, at the edge of the West Side Medical Center. Ashland had been a wealthy "Gold Coast" mansion location fifty years earlier, and the frat houses were located in these rehabilitated old mansions.

Each of the fraternities cited their advantages over student dorm living, since freshmen would be living with experienced, helpful upperclassmen with lots of handy study materials. This week each frat house provided a similar evening party of beer, food, and eager recruiters.

After three years of dorm life, I thought frat house living might be a pleasant and valuable change. We interested freshmen responded, and each received an assignment to visit a different house each night, to assure each frat got a chance to meet every recruit.

I was excited because this invitation indicated – dorm or frat – that I really was in medical school!

Rush Week

So it was a fun, beery week, and exciting to be in the presence of other incoming freshmen, and to be initiated into medical education by upperclassmen. There were about 200 incoming freshmen, almost half from Cook County. The balance were chosen, one from each of Illinois' remaining 101 counties, for the very practical purpose of providing general practitioners for the rural "downstate" counties. There were several international students as well. I guessed that I represented Cook County, having been born in Chicago and lived there for the past three years.

Five or six women were in our class, barely three percent. (Today, women represent

IOTA

OF

PHI BETA PI FRATERNITY

more than fifty percent of the incoming U of I medical class.) Many of the freshmen were married and lived at home in nearby suburbs; perhaps fifty single freshmen lived in the student dorm, other singles lived at home, and maybe sixty freshmen lived in the four fraternity houses.

Each frat had a its own flavor: Alpha Kappa Kappa was said to favor athletes, or "jocks"; Nu Sigma Nu prided itself on its high GPA and intellectual members; Phi Beta Pi was dismissed as a "party house." The fourth, Phi Rho Sigma seemed to attract a lot of effeminate guys, the "joy boys." (At this time, homosexuals – not yet "gays" – were very discreetly "in the closet.")

Despite the "party house" label, Phi Beta Pi seemed warmly wholesome, featuring well-rounded guys with joie de vivre. Bill Watkins, a fun-loving but sincerely helpful Phi Beta Pi senior (or M4), won my heart. I enjoyed partying, and later touring the "Phi Bete" (rhymes with "fly-bait") house with Bill. The house was said to have been the former Wrigley (chewing gum) Mansion, featuring a large third floor ballroom, which had been converted to a 20-bed dormitory.

I met the cook, John Henry Powell, a big, jovial Negro with a booming and infectious laugh, who had been with the frat "for fifty years." John Henry served breakfast and dinner, five days a week. Bill told me there were house jobs available to help defray room and board expenses.

Party House

Frankly, one of the primary attractions of the "Phi Bete" house was the fun! Rip-roaring songs and stories every evening during Rush Week. I couldn't help stopping by nightly on my way home after my other assigned frat house visits: Watkins, Dick Martens, and Monty Maples were opening the beer kegs and leading choruses of bawdy songs, jokes, and limericks, which lent a raucous air of camaraderie to the group. At week's end I could not resist Pledging with Phi BetaPi National Medical Fraternity, and moving into this lively, welcoming house.

Back at Loyola, I closed out my job with Dr. Jaskowski and my beloved rats, after having successfully demonstrated that it was pancreatic digestive enzymes that hatched the worm eggs; now, how to block them from hatching? I packed up my dorm trunk and said goodbye to my Polish Mafia buddies. All were staying for their fourth-year college degree: Allen applying to med school, Stan to dental school, not sure about Charlie or Swierk. I said goodbye to Father Montville, the director, and arranged to have my mail forwarded to the Phi Beta Pi fraternity house at 709 S. Ashland Avenue.

New Bike I

My motorcycle had arrived at his home, so Allen and I uncrated it, filled the fluids, installed a battery, and away I went! After registration, I was able to keep it safely in the small back yard at the frat house.

Thinking about this next move, I reflected that, after leaving home and high school, the Loyola-run dorm was a safe steppingstone along my emerging pathway. Now, moving to an independent, student-run household seemed a little less-secure step; not too slippery, I hoped.

XVIII

ΦΒΣ

Frat Boy

Moving Day

On moving day, Bill Watkins brought a truck to the dorm for my belongings, then helped me move in. Bill gave me the house key and pay-phone number, HAymarket1-9145.

There were nine study rooms in the house, each with two desks. Five or six upperclassmen lived there, and ten or twelve of us freshmen were moving in. Many upper classmen had taken one of eleven coveted Phi Bete externships: room and salary or board (meals) jobs in local hospitals and clinics. Other members were married or lived at home. But they all showed up for parties on the weekends!

Bill assigned me a lower bunk in the third-floor former ballroom, now dormitory. He explained that the upperclassmen often worked nights in the hospitals and slept during the day, so the dorm was kept exclusively for sleeping, with no conversation, no lights, and all the windows painted black. I remember thinking, "Working in the hospital at night – how dramatic!"

"Here is where my medical career will begin," I thought, "in this house of *playful* but very *studious* future doctors." Both those traits suited me well!

Rather than share a study room, I chose the large former wardrobe room at the entrance to the ballroom-dorm. This was a "glorified coat closet" for the Wrigley guests, and measured about 7 by 10 feet, with room for my trunk, plus a bookshelf and small desk. It had a nice window at the far end for light and ventilation. No one had occupied it before, and I preferred solitude. (Little did I realize the room's potential value.)

Hank Reeves, another freshman, and former Navy Medical Corpsman, moved in next, and helped me carry a spare desk up into my room.

Med Center Tour

Before classes began, some of the upperclassmen took us on a walking tour of the

STOP
5 · 10 · 25
U.S. COINS ONLY
COIN RELEASE
payphone.com
Local Calls
PUSH FOR COIN

nearby West Side Medical Center hospitals: huge Cook County Hospital (CCH), Presbyterian (now Rush) St. Luke's Hospital (PSLH), Tuberculosis Sanitorium (TBSan), Hines Veterans' Hospital (VA), Illinois Research and Education (R&E, "rare & exotic"), and our U of Illinois block-long neo-Gothic complex.

One of the upper-class (M4) frat guys was on an obstetrics rotation at Cook County Hospital. He met us and took some of us in to watch when he was called to deliver a baby! We were so excited, feeling like we were on our way to becoming medical doctors!

A fascinating and fulfilling education lay ahead of us!

HISTORICAL NOTE

Telephone Exchanges: Across the U.S. seven-digit phone numbers began with names, called "exchanges" then, such as Broadway, Walnut, etc. The first two letters of the name were capitalized and corresponded to the digits of those two letters on the phone dial. Thus, Haymarket would be 42. (The small letter designations on your cell (or mobile) phone are a remainder from those days.) The system lasted until the mid-sixties, when ten-digit numbers with area codes replaced the old seven-digit system, to serve a growing nation of telephone users.

XIX

MEDICAL EDUCATION

Medical Education in the Sixties

Another of the frat guys explained the plan of our coming medical education. (As I write this sixty years later, I'm aware that there are some minor, or even major, changes in this classic curriculum.)

Pre-Clinical Years

He told us that the first two years are called pre-clinical, mostly lectures and labs. We'd wear short white jackets and civilian clothes. The first year (M1) is devoted to normal human structure and function: anatomy: gross, neuroanatomy and histology (cell anatomy), of every organ. Then physiology (how the organs work and what they do) of all the body's systems: cardiac, neural, pulmonary, digestive, kidney and urogenital, etc.; plus, normal psychiatry.

The second pre-clinical year (M2) would be everything abnormal or injurious to human structure and function, namely pathology of all those organs and systems mentioned above. Then there was pharmacology, microbiology, preventive medicine, and the most fun for us: Physical Diagnosis, where we would carry our little black bags and apply our training and senses to take a careful medical history, then examine patients to diagnose their disorder or disease. (This now-neglected art was critically important before today's advanced lab work and Imaging: CT scans, MRIs, etc.)

At the end of our M2 year we would face two days of The National Board of Medical Examiners, Part I Exam to determine if we were ready for patients in our next two clinical years. It all sounded very exciting, and a little scary. Was I up to it?

Clinical Years

Our final two Clinical years (M3 and M4) would be devoted to direct patient care. We'd wear full whites, be addressed as "doctor," and rotate through clinics representing all the major branches of medicine: surgery (and its subspecialties, orthopedics, urology, otolaryngology, etc.) Then obstetrics/gynecology, internal medicine (with its subspecialties, such as cardiology, gastroenterology, pulmonology, etc.) Then pediatrics, emergency medicine, etc. We'd be under the supervision of interns and residents, who, in turn, were supervised by Attending Physicians or teaching staff.

Internship

At the end of the final year, we would again face The National Board of Medical Examiners, for the Part II exam, to determine if we were competent to proceed to an Internship. There we'd be seeing hospital and clinic patients on our own, relatively unsupervised, to expand our learning and polish our skills.

It all sounded very rewarding, and maybe a little intimidating. But Leon, one of the in-house M4 guys, encouraged me, saying, "It's not about brilliance, John, it's about discipline: keep your ass on your desk chair nightly for long hours, study hard, and you'll make it."

"Besides," he went on, "here at the frat house we have a skull, bones, a complete skeleton, microscope slides, old exams, textbooks, and experienced upperclassmen like me, to coach you and answer questions. Also, we'll give you advice about choosing books, taking lecture notes and tests, and even the personalities of different professors. You'll do just fine!" Leon was certainly reassuring; I still felt mildly uncertain about my abilities, although with discipline and hard work, I'd always been successful – so far!

House Job

At the house I arranged to defray part of my room and board by working as a busboy and dishwasher, helping John Henry Powell in the kitchen. Constantly reciting bad jokes and off-color stories, he was quite a delightful character! We became close friends. John Henry often said, "Stick with pretty women, fast horses, and sportin' men!" His motto was "Live while your eyes are open!" I certainly didn't need much encouragement in that area!

New friends

After Hank Reeves, the next freshman I met was Bruce Fick, who had just graduated from Pharmacy School, and had now decided on med school. Bruce was quiet, earnest, and had a great sense of humor. For tuition Bruce worked weekends as a Registered Pharmacist and proved to be a good man to know. I had fun with an upperclassman, Bill Wittner from Germany, and I enjoyed practicing my German with him. Bill had worked his way through pre-med as a bellboy at the German-run Bismark Hotel in Chicago. His house job was to look after the coal bin in the cellar and keep the furnace burning during the winter and whenever needed.

We took our book lists to the local Login Bros. Medical Books and picked up our short jackets at Mueller's Medical Supply. We were ready to begin our medical education!

XX

Off to "Docker Schoo"

The term "Docker Schoo" was a mildly pejorative put-down on ourselves, lest as medical students we become too prideful.

It was just three or four blocks to our school building, a pleasant walk in this fall weather, although it became a challenge during windy winters. I was so grateful for my big Maxwell Street parka!

As promised, school was mostly lectures at first; we took careful notes and enjoyed our classes. The lecture hall's design was unique: there were perhaps fifty rows of seating arranged very steeply, so that even students in the back of the hall were relatively close to the lecturer and projection screen. This was especially helpful when patients were presented to the class.

We studied the anatomy and physiology of all the organ-systems: cardiac, renal (kidney), respiratory, digestive, neural, etc. We felt pretty special in our white jackets initially, but came to realize that, like the beanies of Loyola college freshmen, these short jackets, in the huge, hierarchical medical center, were a sign of our low-rank status as M1s or M2s.

In histology, we studied blood and tissue microscope slides by the hour, and it was quite fatiguing using my antique monocular microscope. I mentioned this to my dad, and for an early Christmas gift he sent me a beautiful new AO Binocular Microscope he had secured at a big discount from his friend Bob Miller, who sold American Optical instruments and lenses.

"Gross!"

For most of us, gross anatomy was the most interesting of our courses. We were first given a serious talk about respecting our cadavers, who would be our teachers for the coming year. They may have been undistinguished in life, but in death they were truly VIPs! We learned the importance of respecting their tissues, because some of the most delicate, fragile parts would need to be identified later, on examinations. We treated these "instructors" very reverently, and some teams even gave affectionate names to their cadavers.

Big Lab

In the dissection hall there were fifty or more embalmed cadavers, mostly males, in waist-high closed, tank-like containers. Opening the covers raised the cadaver's platform for exposure, and the embalming fluid (chiefly formaldehyde) smell could be quite unpleasant at first. The bodies lay on their backs, wrapped like mummies in oiled muslin to keep them from drying out. We unwrapped only the parts we were dissecting. After my college dissections of frog, cat, pigeon, shark, fish, and even that earthworm, I was certainly comfortable with this dissection.

Some cadavers had been donated by the deceased individual or his family, others were unclaimed from Cook County Morgue, or were alcoholics collected from Chicago's back streets, where they had passed out, then frozen in winter.

Cadaver Team

Four of us were assigned to each cadaver, two standing on a side, appointed alphabetically. This is where I met and made friendships with Coniglio, Cope, and Cowen.

Week after week, we four worked together, carefully dissecting and identifying every nerve, blood vessel, muscle and tendon, alongside a greasy Gray's Anatomy textbook.

Stressful Exams

Every month or so, there would be a practical exam, where a numbered tag would be placed on each cadaver, in the areas we had been dissecting. These tags were attached to a nerve, muscle, blood vessel, tendon, or other structure, and we moved from one cadaver to the next with a clipboard and blank numbered answer sheet. We were given sixty seconds to identify and record each item, then a bell rang and we moved to the next cadaver, and so forth, around the room to answer all fifty cadaver questions. There were additional stations with microscope slides, for us to identify different organs and tissues.

If I couldn't identify the cadaver tag or tissue slide before the bell rang, I might guess or leave it blank, but couldn't go back to look. If I delayed, pondering at the cadaver, Ding! The student behind would bump me forward, so he could have his full 60 seconds at that cadaver. The pressure to move ahead, identify the item, write it down, and move forward when the bell rang, Ding! Set a rather grueling pace, reminding me of Dr. Spiroff and our difficult worm dissection at Loyola.

These "practicals" could be even more stressful. Here's an example of "Haste makes waste": If on the cadaver rotation, I wasn't certain what tissue number 10 was, I'd leave the line blank and move on to identify cadaver number 11. Ding! I might then hastily put that answer on the next open line, Ding! and hurry on to number 12 when the bell rang. Ding! Maybe five or six stations later, I'd recall number 10, but when trying to enter it, I realized that I had mistakenly put the answer for 11 on that previously blank line for 10! Ding! Oh, no! So, the last half-dozen answers were each on the wrong line! They'll all be marked wrong! Ding! Oh, my God! Then followed the frantic erasing, recalling, and rewriting, Ding! While trying to keep up! Ding!

If a student were trembling with the pressure while holding a tag, it might accidentally be torn off the delicate nerve or vessel, making it impossible for everyone following him to identify any structure. I often finished the exam in a cold sweat. Next month there would be another gross anatomy "practical" from another location on the body, with different tagged tissues.

Body Donation

We spent the full M1 year carefully dissecting and identifying every part of our guy, inside and out; he taught us so much! (Since I've been a teacher most of my life, I've donated my own remains to our local med school as well, so I can keep teaching after I've "shed my mortal coil" and have no further use for it.)

Dad's Eye Chart

Dad's Japanese Chinese eye chart had become popular for use with elderly Asian patients. He sent me this clipping.

A Chinese Japanese Projectochart Slide

PHILIP M. CORBOY, M.D., HONOLULU

WHEN MY JAPANESE PROJECTOCHART slide was introduced in August of 1956,[1] it was evident in the practice of ophthalmology in Honolulu and other similarly populated centers, which are multilingual, and in which a large segment of the population are of oriental extraction, that to properly test vision with Japanese who were not familiar with English characters currently employed (Snellen), it was necessary to provide a test slide using Japanese characters. That Projectochart slide, per se, functioned to great advantage.

Subsequently, it has been found that among other oriental races, the Chinese and Koreans particularly, that a Projectochart slide using their characters also was highly desirable. This need has given place to the design and production of a new Projectochart slide[2] which has been divided into two halves, one Chinese characters, which also can be used by Koreans, the other half Japanese characters, which are easily understood by both Japanese and Okinawans.

The requirements of Snellen type, i.e., that the characters subtend an angle of 5 minutes of arc, have been adhered to with great accuracy.

Characters varying from 20/300 to 20/15 are now available in stepdown sizes. There are quite a number of characters that are common to both Chinese and Japanese, and this fact was taken advantage of by using only one such common character for the 20/300 line, two such for the 20/200 line, and four for the 20/100 line on the projectochart slide.

The 20/80 line in this new slide is unique in that it contains a built-in bichromatic testing facility. The left half of the line is red, the right half green, on which have been superimposed four equal circles or Landolt's rings, which fit evenly into the projected square of the image on the screen, and which do not necessitate the addition of a colored filter being drawn over them. This facilitates quick use of the bichromatic testing function, with disregard to either oriental characters, and without loss of time by the examiner.

Below the 20/80 line, are eight lines of evenly numbered and divided characters. Chinese and Japanese, ranging from 20/70 to 20/15 inclusive.

JUNE, 1960 29

Dad's Eye Chart described in a local Asian newspaper.

Follow Advice

In the lecture hall I learned lessons about test preparation. In one case, Renal (kidney) Physiology, I became very interested in electrolyte balance maintained by the kidney, and – against the advice of an upperclassman – I got "carried away", spending far too much time investigating conflicting details in several different renal textbooks.

On the final exam I was stunned to realize that the questions were taken almost verbatim from the lectures of the professor, a renowned renal expert. I studied all the wrong stuff. I got a D in the course, became quite discouraged (after all my detailed research) and was called into the Dean's office to explain my poor grade.

I was so disappointed, ashamed, even embarrassed, that for a brief time I was somewhat depressed. (I began to wonder if this Medicine was too much for me; maybe I should drop out and join the Air Force?) I've never been troubled by depression, and so this quickly passed, and I realized the problem wasn't stupidity, but simply my poor approach to exam-taking. My friends who had studied only the lecture notes did very well and from then on, I learned to follow advice, especially from upperclassmen.

Back in the frat house, we all spent four or five hours nightly, quietly reviewing the day's notes, slides, bones, etc. It was clear that even these very smart guys were being really challenged to absorb everything. Me, too!

Mnemonic Fun

There was a great camaraderie, putting our heads together studying each night.

Mnemonics were memory aids that came in handy. For example, the twelve pairs of cranial nerves are recalled by the classic: "On Old Olympus' Towering Tops, A Finn and German Viewed Some Hops." Each first letter brings to mind the first letter of one of the twelve cranial nerve pairs: Olfactory, Optic, Oculomotor, Trochlear, Trigeminal, Abducens, Facial, Acoustic, Glossopharyngeal, Vagus, Spinal accessory, and Hypoglossal.

Biochemistry was perhaps the most challenging for many of us, and Hank Reeves was a wizard at creating his own humorous mnemonics. For the B vitamins, Thiamine, Riboflavin, Niacin, Pantothenic acid, Pyridoxine, Biotin, Folate, Cyano-Cobalamin, his unforgettable mnemonic was "Two Rubber Nuts Prove Pretty Bad for Christmas." But it worked: I also still remember after 60 years Hank's mnemonic for disaccharides: Maltose, Cellobiose, Lactose, Sucrose, was "Mother Crotch Loves Sucrose" (Decades later at frat reunions, we've enjoyed hilariously recalling "the undying love of Mother Crotch for Sucrose!")

Some subjects were best handled by studying together in pairs or small groups, comparing notes and pearls (brilliant insights). Other subjects, requiring sheer rote memory or deep comprehension, I preferred to tackle alone in my big coat closet, which I named Toad Hall (from *Wind in the Willows*), and painted that title on my door.

XXI

SOCIAL LIFE

House Parties

Quiet and studious as our "school nights" were, the weekends were an entirely different matter. There was a nice restaurant called The Greek's, across the street from Cook County Hospital, for dinner dates. But with our limited budgets more often on a Saturday night a group of us from the house, joined by some of the single members living at home, would go to a casual bar called The Owl's where we could meet and dance with girls from nearby Cook County School of Nursing dormitory. After a few drinks and dances, we'd each choose a lady, then we'd invite her back to the frat house for more drinks and dancing, and perhaps to come upstairs to tour the house or visit our rooms.

At the house, the girls often reminded us that they had an eleven PM curfew at their school dormitory. One of our upperclassmen routinely set our living room clock back an hour on weekends, so unsuspecting ladies belatedly realized that they had overstayed and missed their curfew. They'd have to choose between facing demerits by returning late, or staying overnight on our living room couches for breakfast. Most chose the late return, but the more adventurous stayed over. (They each had a nurse's wristwatch, however, so maybe they chose to stay over?)

To take advantage of the situation, I bought a narrow, three by seven-foot dining table from a used furniture place, then got a Thrift Store mattress, sheets, and pillows, to create a very comfortable, somewhat narrow, tabletop bed within the privacy of Toad Hall. I had my dormitory bed for sleeping, but I envisioned the Toad Hall "bed" might be for entertaining.

Nematode Surprise!

One day I happened to glance into the toilet after a bowel movement, and saw a familiar sight: a foot-long Ascaris lumbricoides roundworm, the kind I had been working with at Loyola. My former intestinal resident. Despite all my caution, hand washing and gloving, somehow I had inadvertently ingested one or more of the invisible eggs which hatched, entered my bloodstream, wormed through my lungs, was coughed up, swallowed and grown in my small intestine, then taken up residence in my colon! Yucky! Imagine a worm living inside you! The next day I went to Student Health and was assured that probably I only had this one, although they took stool samples for eggs and worms, which turned out negative.

Quite a surprise finding this post-resident of my colon!

XXII

Take a Break

Christmas '59

Soon it was Christmas break. I flew home to tell my family all about med school. Unfortunately, Shirley was no longer in Hawaii. After her '57 graduation from Sacred Hearts, her dad was transferred to the Coast Guard base in Florida, where I had visited her last spring in Miami. Waikiki Beach just wasn't the same, without Shirley.

Water-Skiing

Without Shirley to play with, I had more free time and learned to water-ski with John Parks and friends. I started with the usual two skis, but soon got pretty good at slalom-skiing. It was great fun, until our friends sold the boat.

ER Adventures

Business at his downtown office had slowed, and Dad bought the Waikiki practice of Dr. Donald Depp, who was retiring. There was little medical insurance then, so people seldom visited a doctor for routine visits or check-ups: usually only if they felt really in need. While establishing his new practice, Dad was working part-time in the Eye Department at Kaiser Foundation Hospital near Waikiki, to fill a vacancy for them.

Since Dad had a connection with Kaiser, one night I visited their Emergency Room, introduced myself as an M1, and offered to help where I could. Two great ER MDs, Willis Butler and Bill Carter, put me to work learning clinical skills. They taught me to take brief medical histories, draw blood and start intravenous (IV) fluids. I learned to apply casts to fractures, read some x-rays, and even suture wounds! It was a magnificent clinical experience for a mere M1 newbie, working every night as a volunteer. I almost hated to go back to a lecture hall: this was *real* medicine!

Thanks, Will and Bill!

January, '60

Soon I was back in Chicago for my second semester as an M1. The school routine was similar to the preceding semester: hard work all week, then recreation on weekends.

Jan G.

One Saturday evening at The Owl's I met a delightful young Cook County Nursing student from Sheboygan, Wisconsin, Jan G. She was a tall, lean, blue-eyed blond and we quickly became weekend party pals. Before long, she enjoyed ignoring curfew and visiting me overnight in Toad Hall. She explained that when she returned to school the following morning, she'd pick up a newspaper and carry it into the dorm. Passing the front desk, she'd hold up the front page, and comment vigorously about the headline, acting as though she had just stepped out to get the morning news. Her ruse worked because she was never questioned.

Soon, we were steady companions every Saturday night in my narrow Toad Hall table-bed. I'd place beer and sandwiches outside on my window ledge, and the chilly weather acted as a refrigerator. With beer and snacks – and me – handy, Jan realized there was no reason to return to the dorm on Sunday morning; she could do the same newspaper act on Monday morning, just as easily. So, we'd also enjoy Sundays together. On a few occasions, when my studies allowed, we began our private party on Friday night, spending entire three-night happy weekends in Toad Hall!

This was my first *intimate* relationship, and the multi-orgasmic Jan could not be happier! When she went home for Easter break, she returned with several famous Sheboygan (German) Summer Sausages, which we enjoyed with our beer on those long romantic weekends.

"I really love this sausage," I once told Jan.

"Mmm, I like yours lots better!" she giggled.

"Coalbin" Wittner

The frat house parties continued through the spring, and sometimes our living room was filled with married guys and their wives, along with single guys with nursing students from The Owl's. I had some bottles of Absolute Alcohol (99.9% ethanol) previously retrieved from Dr. Jaskowski's lab. This is 200 proof alcohol, which I used to dehydrate tissues to stain them for microscope slides. This pure Neutral Spirits was tasteless and odorless, but really powerful. To keep costs down, a pint of this stuff in the punchbowl could create a pleasantly strong drink. Because it was tasteless, the guys usually cautioned their dates, but sometimes the girls would guzzle and get too much *punch*! Occasionally, even the guys, who should know better, forgot and went too far.

One chilly night, Bill Wittner excused himself mid-party, and left his date in the living room, while he went to the cellar to stoke the furnace. After he failed to return, his date asked someone to check on him. I think it was Norm Aves who went down and found Bill passed out, lying in the coal bin. Norm let him sleep it off, explaining to the perplexed young lady that Bill had fallen asleep but was okay. Some of the girls returning to the dorm walked her home.

The next morning at breakfast Bill stumbled upstairs – completely covered in coal dust – black from head to foot, except for two bloodshot eyes! It was a sight terrifying enough to confirm good judgment in having left him downstairs the night before, lest he return in the middle of the party, looking like a zombie!

Typical spider monkey like mine.

XXIII

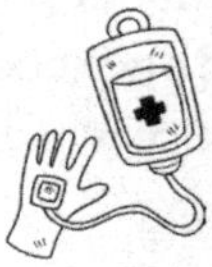

Extracurricular Activities

Monkey Business

Early in the semester I had bought a spider monkey, although only God knows what motivated me. He lived with us in the fraternity house. He ran free in the house and loved to race up and down three flights of stairs by leaping on the banisters. We fed him table scraps and some monkey food, but he seemed to be hungry most of the time.

Taking him to the backyard morning, afternoon, and night, I trained him to pee and poop outdoors. Most of the time.

He liked to chew on the paint of the banisters for some reason, and later we learned that this is usually caused by some malnutrition, and the chewing condition is called pica.

The problem with chewing on the old paint was that it likely had a high lead content, and before long he was demonstrating the textbook symptoms of lead poisoning. To keep him away from paint-chewing, I let him live in our backyard on a long leash, where he enjoyed swinging on our clotheslines. One day I returned from school to find he had been twisting in the clotheslines, got himself tangled in the ropes and leash, and had strangled! Adios, pal!

Blood for Beer

One of the upperclassmen told us that there was a blood laboratory not far away, where we could sell our blood plasma. I went over to investigate and learned that the lab was creating anti-sera (antibody-rich serum). At that time, they were producing cobra anti-venom. They would give me a shot of dilute cobra venom, and my body would create antibodies against this poisonous venom. After three weeks they would collect and refine my serum for use as emergency treatment for cobra bite victims.

I agreed to try it, so I took the painful injection. It made me a little sick for a day or two, then I recovered. I returned in three weeks, when my blood was loaded with antibodies. They drew a pint of my blood, then spun it down to separate the red cells from the plasma. My red cells were returned to me in the IV, and my plasma was used to create anti-venom for emergency treatment of cobra bites. This serum draw could be repeated monthly, for so long as my antibodies were being produced. After that I could get another cobra's sting, but I decided one venomous poisoning was enough. For this we got $20 per visit, so I collected $100, which went toward the Toad Hall weekend refreshments.

Later I returned for a similar procedure. The same routine was now being used to make blood-typing serum: first, we were injected with a foreign blood type. For example, I am type A, so received blood type B, and my body made antibodies against that type. After several weeks, my anti-B plasma was drawn and used to make blood typing serum. This routine earned the same $20 per visit, but was much easier to endure, and garnered another hundred bucks. Several friends went monthly for other profitable programs, until we future doctors learned that it was probably not a good idea to continually challenge our immune systems this way.

Foreign Student?

One day that spring I was called to the office of the Bursar, Mr. Moon. He said, "John, there's been a mistake in your tuition. As an international student, you are not eligible for either the non-state tuition or the Illinois resident rate." I was familiar with the term, international student, since Bill Wittner was from Germany, and my M1 frat brother Paco Rojas was from Costa Rica. But me, from Hawaii? International? I wondered, how could that be?

Moon explained that since I was from Hawaii, I was admitted as a foreign student, and should be paying the higher tuition rate. I protested that Hawaii was a U.S. Territory and not a foreign country, but to no avail. He even wanted me to pay the higher rate for the past semester as well. I had received the first-year scholarship from the Pullman Foundation, but was reluctant to ask for additional funds.

I wrote this disappointing news to my dad, who coughed up the additional funds, but urged me to file a formal request for state residency, to get the tuition back down for the next year, when the Pullman Foundation funding expired. Mr. Moon offered to write Indianapolis, to procure the forms I'd require to apply for State Residency.

Professional Courtesy

One of my frat brothers told me he'd had dental work done for free at the local Dental School. I had a couple of annoying wisdom teeth, and so I booked an appointment. Students extracted all four of my wisdom teeth at one sitting, supervised by instructors; I was later advised that this was inappropriate, and to avoid complications, I should have had extractions in only one jaw at a time.

I also learned that we medical students could get free haircuts, courtesy of the nearby Barber College. Most of us took advantage of this opportunity, and tipped the students, although occasionally our haircuts looked noticeably amateurish.

XXIV

LOOKING AHEAD

Work Week

Bill Watkins gave us some instructions about preparing for Rush Week at the end of the summer, making plans for welcoming the incoming freshmen with food and beer.

He explained that the week before that, all frat members, whether living in or out of the house, are expected to show up for Work Week, when the house would receive a complete top to bottom deep cleaning: washing windows and walls; painting and repairing of necessary items; cleaning carpets, drapes, and couches; and a general sprucing-up before the freshmen arrived. Bill asked if I would take charge of the week's procedures. I am a pretty good organizer, and it sounded simple enough, so I agreed.

Job Opportunity?

Bill told me that there were almost a dozen outside jobs available exclusively to Phi Bete M3s and M4s, which were arranged through the kindness of various fraternity alumni. These usually included free room and a small salary at certain medical offices and clinics. Even better were room and board externships (no salary) at some hospitals and emergency rooms around town. M2s were encouraged to take these jobs when becoming M3s, to make room in the frat house for incoming freshmen.

Bill said that one of our M4 frat brothers with a room and board job at the Illinois Eye and Ear Infirmary (IEEI) was being married this summer and would be moving out of the Infirmary. Might I be interested?

I think Bill offered me this opportunity because I had agreed to handle Work Week for him. Bill said he thought I was doing well enough in school that I could live out of the house as an M2. He believed I was sufficiently responsible to represent the fraternity well, in order to retain the job for future Phi Beta Pi brothers. He promised that I could take the vacancy when it became available. Naturally, I was thrilled when I learned that five frat guys lived there, and the job provided room, meals, and laundry for performing non-medical, clerical work.

One of my chief concerns was that by leaving the frat house, I'd lose access to my dear Toad Hall, and those glorious intimate weekends with Jan in our lovely private boudoir. But the opportunity and financial advantages would be worth trying to figure something out for continuing our weekend relationship.

My hot BMW R-69 S, top of the line.

New Bike II

Sometime during that semester, I realized that my BMW one-cylinder, 250cc bike did not furnish the pep I needed, so I traded up at a dealer in Aurora for a BMW two-cylinder 600cc R-69. What a difference in power and speed! The two cylinders ("boxer twins") were horizontally opposed, each with its own carburetor, a feature of BMWs. Since the cylinders were out in the airstream, they ran cooler, which permitted higher compression ratios, satisfying my urge for more power – and even prestige.

Alumni Flight

During second semester I was working hard, getting satisfactory grades, and looking forward to summer break. A notice was posted at school announcing that a charter round trip flight to Europe for alumni this coming summer had been under-booked. The low charter fare depended on a full flight, so faculty and students were invited to join alumni on the trip. I was eager to visit my friends in Germany again, so when I learned there was an opening, I canceled my summer plans for Hawaii. When the semester ended, I took the very reasonably priced flight.

Fire!

It's a bit of a blur exactly where I went and what I did with my German family and friends, because in the middle of the summer I received notice that our beloved fraternity house had burned down! It was hard to believe: suddenly, we had no home! But through phone calls I learned that our fraternity alumnus, Dr. McCormick, had rallied Chicago alumni to raise money to purchase or lease another old mansion. Our "new" house was just across the street at 806 South Ashland Avenue. The alums would pay for renovation materials, if we boys would do the hard work.

Big Work "Week"

Therefore, my easy Work Week job would require almost three tough weeks. On my return from Europe, we pitched in immediately, with almost all the frat brothers, remodeling and renovating to prepare the house in time for Rush Week.

I became the "general contractor": the alums rented a truck and hired an electrician and plumber to wire and plumb multiple study rooms. I was put in charge while carpenters helped to turn each large upstairs bedroom into two smaller study bedrooms. We salvaged and installed some kitchen equipment from the ruins of the old house. Most guys really pitched in, working 16-hour days for almost three full weeks. I delivered the beer every afternoon at five, followed later by sandwiches and popular Italian sausage plates, to keep the boys plastering, painting, flooring, plumbing, and carpeting all evening. Alumni wives purchased and delivered furnishings, including twenty beds, desks, study lamps and much more.

Lesson Learned

During the final week, I was pushing the guys pretty hard, scolding, "C'mon, guys, less beer-chatting, more working!" And worse. There was some quiet grumbling about my "slave driver" approach. Bill Watkins took me aside:

"John," he said, "These guys are volunteers. Many have been here since 7am! They are working to please you. I know you're tireless and under pressure to finish the house in time, but you've got to lighten up, or you'll lose them! Praise and appreciation will get more done than orders and criticism: try it."

Bill was right, of course: I mended my ways, more work got done, and we finished in time! Thanks, Bill.

We all had worked tirelessly to pull the "new" house together. I was really impressed by the guys' camaraderie and talent. What an amazing transformation of the house! The paint was still drying when the incoming Rush Week freshmen arrived. Whew! But we made it, and the rush parties that week were just as fun and boisterous as those at the old house.

The Illinois Charitable Eye and Ear Infirmary, at Chicago.

Built 1874

The venerable Illinois Eye and Ear Infirmary, where my father – and I – both lived for three years. (Courtesy University of Illinois Archives)

XXV

INFIRMARY FUTURE

New Home

By Rush Week '60, I learned that the IEEI job had indeed opened up, so I recruited some help to move into the third floor Residents' Quarters of the Illinois Eye and Ear Infirmary, 904 West Adams, not far from the Medical Center. (At one time, all specialist trainees actually resided within the hospital where they were being trained, thus the designation, *residents*.)

At this time, most residents were married and living elsewhere, and the rooms – except for one "resident on-call" room – were given over to us student workers.

Insurance Lesson

My clothing had all been lost in the fire, since my trunk, although salvaged, had been soaked with water by the fire fighters, and most of the contents were ruined. My dad helped me file a claim on our family fire insurance policy, so I got a modest cash settlement to buy myself some clothes. I learned something about insurance claims: for example, my very nice, hundred dollar suit, because it was five years old (but hardly worn), it was said by the insurance company to have depreciated 80 percent, to only be worth $20. But of course, $20 wouldn't buy me another suit! And so on, similar compensation for the rest of my ruined wardrobe.

The Job

My roommate at the Infirmary was my pal, "Coal bin" Bill Wittner, so I was enjoying some German language again. Bill was now an M4, and had moved into the infirmary the preceding June.

Bill explained that the evening job for the five of us was filing the several hundred medical charts from the day's clinic patients, in time for the next day's clinic. For this reason, all the charts needed to be properly filed every night. Each evening we divided the piles of charts into five equal stacks. If one of us was not on the job, it would fall to the others to deal with his share. In this way we regularly covered for one another as needed.

In addition, we were responsible for handling the Infirmary switchboard on weekends. Bill soon taught me both jobs, which we shared equally among the five of us. He explained the cafeteria hours and its generally good, free "institutional food". He introduced me to the Administrator, state employee Lester Gerber, whom I thanked for the opportunity, and pledged to do my very best. Bill also pointed out that since I'd soon be wearing "full whites" to hospitals and clinics, the free, near-professional laundry service was invaluable!

Fall '60

We began the semester as M2s, and after our year of *normal* human structure and function, it was a joy to begin our more-interesting courses in *abnormal* structure and function of the human body. This included Pathology of diseased or injured organs and tissues, and the processes that harmed or damaged them, whether infectious, chemical, cancerous, traumatic, nutritional, or environmental, etc. We worked through the pathology of all the organs and systems: heart and lungs; liver and gallbladder; pancreas and intestines; kidney and reproductive organs; blood, lymphatic, and hormonal; brain and neurological; sensory and musculoskeletal, etc.

In Microbiology we were introduced to bacteria and viruses, "the bugs that bug us," and to Pharmacology, learning the means for easing symptoms, preventing or treating disease. Then there was Preventive Medicine. The days and nights were long, and the material was voluminous. The practical exams included microscope slides of blood, urine, spinal fluid, and tissues, along with jars of diseased or damaged organs.

Elective

We were offered an opportunity to choose an elective this year. I chose to work with one of the endocrinologists, but switched to Dr. Sydney Kaufman, an oncologist, who offered me a thousand-dollar stipend if I could create a hollow model of a spinal vertebra for use in evaluating radiotherapy dosing. I put my former Polish Mafia pal, Stan Kaczala, to the task: he made me a perfect life-size, clear plastic, hollow, lumbar vertebra model in his Dental School Lab! I gave him half my stipend, and Dr. Kaufman was very pleased with the result.

Path Presentations

Sometimes patients were presented to the class to demonstrate a pathological condition. I remember fascinating cases of brain damage where various interconnections were lost. One patient, presented by a neurologist, sat before us in the lecture hall, and was shown a banana. He looked at it carefully but was completely unable to identify it.

"Is it a banana?" asked the instructor.

"No way," the patient replied. Then the neurologist handed it to him: holding the banana, the patient was immediately able to shout, "That's easy! It is a banana."

Another patient was blindfolded, then handed an apple. He carefully turned it around in his hands, smelled it, and even took a bite, but was unable to identify the

fruit until his blindfold was removed:
"Oh, it's an apple!"
Fascinating neuropathology.

XXVI

Real Patients

Physical Diagnosis

The most interesting part of this M2 year was our course in Physical Diagnosis (or "PDog.") Our same alphabetic cadaver team of Coniglio, Cope, Corboy and Cowen met weekly with Dr. Dean Dimick at the Hines Veterans' Hospital, where we learned to take a complete medical history. We started with the CC: Chief Complaint ("What brings you here today?"); HPI: History of the present illness ("Tell me details about this problem"); PMH: Past medical history ("What medical and surgical issues have you had in the past?"); FH: Family history ("How about the health of your parents and siblings? What diseases run in your family?"). This was followed by general questions regarding medications, allergies, etc.

History Fun

Occasionally we enjoyed a little levity, provided by the interesting answers to our inquiries: One lady told me she refused surgery for her "Fireballs of the uterus" (fibroids), but she did have a successful operation on her "very close veins" (varicose). Another lady said, "The doctor told me I had 'a cute agina'" (acute angina).

One of my frat brothers told of a patient who had been treated for "severe flea bites" (phlebitis) and "sore eyes on my elbows" (psoriasis). Another had suffered "Smilin' mighty Jesus." He had to review the chart to learn it was spinal meningitis. Some conditions were truly confounding, as when a case of "…somethin' like 'Merkety-tikety-tok'" was later revealed to be Meckel's Diverticulum. There were many more, some unprintable.

Physical Examination

This history was followed by a complete physical exam. First, we learned to take and record the vital signs, T, P, R, BP: temperature, pulse, respirations, and blood pressure. After this we were taught the tools of a physical exam: First, *inspection* of the patient and the object of his chief complaint. This was followed by *palpation*, where we felt the affected body part(s): hard or soft, tender, throbbing or pulsating. Then there was *auscultation*, where we listened with the stethoscope to the sounds of heartbeat, blood flow, lungs, and bowels. Finally, there was *percussion*, tapping on the chest or belly to hear whether it was hollow like lung air or intestinal gas, or solid like liver or fluid; then tapping tendons with a little rubber hammer to test the reflexes.

We never forget the five signs of inflammation: redness, warmth, swelling, pain, and loss of function, of which even the ancients were well aware: in the well-known Latin they are listed as "rubor, calor, tumor, dolor, et functio laesa."

Four years of high school Latin was certainly helpful with learning medicine, but a semester of Medical Terminology might have been as good, if not better.

Then we carefully recorded our findings from the history and physical, so that we could come up with a presumptive diagnosis, or specify what additional information we needed from laboratory work: blood, urine, x-ray, etc.

All our findings were then discussed with our teacher, Dr. Dimick, who praised what we discovered and showed us what we had missed. Then he assigned us plenty of patients in the hospital to visit, performing our physical exam to see what an arthritic joint or a cirrhotic liver or consolidated pneumonia lung looked like, felt like, or sounded like during our physical exam. Every patient provided a fun, deductive challenge.

State Resident

Once school got underway, Mr. Moon provided me with forms for applying to Springfield for my Illinois State Residency. I stated that I was born in Illinois, had lived in Chicago for the past three years, and had relatives who were Chicagoland natives. I had an Illinois driver's license (in addition to John Kloppenburg's), and Chicago voter and library cards. One unexpected question was whether I had left the state at any time in the past three years. I fibbed, ignoring the preceding summer's alumni charter trip. I felt this lie was risky, because they might be aware of my school trip, but apparently no one noticed, or a vacation tour was not what the question was seeking. Within a few weeks, I received the paperwork which I presented to Mr. Moon, who put me into the state resident tuition category. Dad and I were pleased, and so was Mr. Moon.

Joke

But the joke was on all of us: Hawaii had been admitted to the Union a year earlier, in August 1959. So, for a full year I was no longer a student from a "foreign country" and had qualified for the US non-Illinois tuition rate. However, this very welcome new Illinois Resident certificate put me in the lowest tuition category of all.

New Bike III

My cadaver pal Dave Cope had joined our fraternity and moved into our "new" frat house this fall. We both shared an interest in motorcycles and took some weekend trips together on his BSA and my BMW. After several of these trips I upgraded my BMW R-69 to a used R-69 S (Sport), which was the top of the line, with 20% more horsepower (from higher compression and larger carburetors) than my previous bike.

When one of our M4s moved out of the Infirmary upon his graduation, Bill Wittner took his place in the solo room, and I promptly nominated Dave Cope to fill the job. He moved in with me over Christmas, and we shared the room for the duration. Our pharmacist pal, Bruce Fick, had moved from the old house to the "new" house after the fire. Bill, Dave, and I joined Bruce and our other brothers at the great weekend frat house parties that fall.

Romantic Reunion

While I was away that summer, Jan had graduated from nursing school and received her Registered Nurse certification. At this time, it was easy to lose track of someone when they moved, since people only had a residence telephone. If they moved somewhere else, that former number was useless, and you could easily lose them. We both had new homes and phone numbers, so it took a while to find each other, usually through mutual friends. Jan had taken a job at Passavant Hospital on the north side of town and was living there. We were both so thrilled when I reached her! She invited me to her single room in the Passavant Nurses' Apartments, and the following weekend we enjoyed an amazing around-the-clock, rollicking reunion!

Jan listed me as a guest/relative, so there was no problem visiting her almost every weekend, regularly parking my motorcycle overnight behind the hospital building. When fall turned to winter, driving on icy streets was tricky, and I often had to ride slowly with both my boots on the ice to avoid slipping over. If it snowed overnight, I'd have to dig my bike out from a snow drift behind the building. After being buried all night in the frozen snow, my bike was often difficult to start. So, while shivering in the gusty winds, I'd pour ether into the carburetors, which always brought the engine quickly to life, for the bone-chilling ride home.

Polish Christmas

I spent Christmas Break '60 in Chicago and enjoyed a reunion with Allen Zencka from my Loyola "Polish Mafia." He had begun his first year at Creighton University Medical School, so we had lots to talk about, and I enjoyed the cultural fun of a Polish Christmas with his family.

Spring '61

Through the winter and into the spring I continued my regular weekend visits to Passavant, which were very fulfilling for Jan and me. Looking back, I realize this was a unique relationship: mostly carnal. Jan joked, "I'm bed-ridden all weekend!" We snacked and sipped, laughed and sang, told stories and read to one another. But we never went out for a meal or a movie. It seems that this simple fun, cuddling together, was all we both wanted. Or all I had time for.

Our second semester as M2s passed all too quickly and finished with the National Board of Medical Examiners Part I: two long days of written and multiple-choice

Inspiring statuette gift from a friend.

exams to determine our readiness for the coming clinical training. Wittner and other upperclassmen had given us some good advice regarding preparation; we all did well and were promoted to M3 in our upcoming clinical year next fall.

Summer '61

I spent the summer at the Infirmary with a couple of the other guys, to keep the medical charts moving and the weekend switchboard covered. We enjoyed kidding around on late nights at the switchboard. When a call came in, Dave loved to answer, "Illin-eye and ear Infirmary..." Or sometimes, "Ill-annoying ear Infirmary..." Even, "Ilin-eyes and ears.."

Bill "Coal bin" Wittner had graduated, and moved out of the Infirmary to get married, so we brought Bruce Fick in from the frat house to take his place. Dave and I took several bike trips together. We once went to Southern Illinois visiting lady friends, former Infirmary employees, and had some fun, beery adventures.

Biker Brotherhood

On one of these trips, while returning to Chicago we passed a biker bar on the South Side and decided it was time for a beer. We pulled over and parked out front with perhaps thirty big Harley bikes. We pushed open the door, stepped in, and, as our eyes adjusted to the dimly-lit bar room, we froze in surprise: the room was packed with large Black bikers! Every head turned to look at us! We were two naïve and vulnerable White boys, entering their exclusive "biker bar" space. Sensing that an abrupt retreat would not be appropriate, we gamely bellied up to the bar, ordered our beers, and greeted the guys next to us. They appeared intimidating, but were cordial, and once we made it clear that we were fellow bikers, it seemed that the "ice was broken" and immediately we were all part of a biker brotherhood.

We enjoyed polite bike-talk and a couple biker stories but didn't hang around for another beer. Whew!

I'd have loved to hear the conversation in that bar as we rode off. And I wondered what the reception would have been, had the roles been reversed, and two naïve young Black bikers had stumbled into a White biker bar. I'd bet the story would be the same: it's a brotherhood, after all.

Full whites

XXVII

CLINICAL YEARS

Clinical Training!

That fall of 1961 was what we'd been waiting years for: we became "clinical clerks" (M3s). We wore full white uniforms, were addressed as "doctor," and carried our little black bags. We rotated through all the services in clinics and hospitals on a 21-month plan. We served several months on Internal Medicine (including psychiatry, cardiology, gastro-enterology, dermatology, allergy, etc); then Obstetrics and Gynecology; as well as Pediatrics. We spent six months on Surgery, since it was broken down into subspecialties, such as urology, orthopedics, ear nose and throat, etc. As M3s, so proud now to be in full white uniforms.

Disappointment

One of our fraternity brothers, Sam Cardinal, had been very uncomfortable during last semester's Physical Diagnosis Course. It seemed that touching patients and feeling or examining their symptomatic parts was very stressful for him, to the point where he was often unable to continue the patient's physical exam.

Sam was one of the brightest of our frat brothers, regularly getting all A's on his pre-clinical work. Despite pep talks from some of his brother upperclassmen, this was a deep-seated phobia that nobody could help Sam with.

Despite all the prior pre-med screening, and the admission interview that were intended to anticipate such situations, Sam's problem had not been foreseen. Sam apparently had no problems with handling and dissecting dead creatures, but this was his first actual contact with warm flesh and blood, and he simply could not handle it. Sam knew that the impending two clinical years would be devoted to physical examinations, touching patients to diagnose their symptoms and physical findings, even performing some invasive procedures on them. Sam had discovered that the practice of medicine requires more than purely intellectual gifts and realized that he simply could not continue. At this point he dropped out and withdrew from med school. We later learned he had secured a job in a medical research lab, where his pre-clinical training proved very valuable.

Junior "Doctors"

In one pocket of my clinic jacket I carried a paperback, Physicians' Handbook, which was loaded with general information, laboratory values, medication dosages, differential diagnoses, etc. In the other pocket I carried the paperback pertaining to the service I was on, such as Pediatric Handbook, Obstetrics and Gynecology Handbook, etc. I prudently avoided consulting these manuals in the presence of the patients.

Foolishness

Despite all the appearances of mature young physicians, we were still young guys subject to foolishness. One night during a party with my classmates the subject of Juarez came up somehow. It was pointed out that it was 1500 miles away and I bragged, "Well, that's not much of a bike ride." One of my friends blurted, "Oh yeah? I'll bet you $100 you wouldn't ride to Juarez." "You're on!", I said, and threw on my jacket, jumped on my bike, and began the long night ride to Juarez. After about 200 miles, I had breakfast south of Peoria, filled my gas tank, and began to calculate the cost of food and fuel to cover the remaining 1300 miles. Now that I was sober and rational it was clear that it would probably cost me more than $100 to get to Juarez and back. I turned around and returned to Chicago by sunrise with my "tail between my legs," the object of considerable laughter among my earlier partygoers. I cleaned up and resumed my clinical duties, none the worse for foolishness.

Inpatients

At teaching hospitals in the medical center, patients were advised upon admission that they'd be seen by a series of doctors to give them the best care. Many seemed to enjoy all the attention.

In the hospital, on each of our services, we were usually the first to see the patient, performing their initial history and physical and writing up our initial evaluation. This was then reviewed by the assigned intern, who next saw the patient, checked our findings, and wrote the admitting orders. He was in turn supervised by the resident or by the patient's Attending Physician (private doctor).

These "Attendings" often provided invaluable impromptu mini-lectures and practical suggestions, based on their years of "real world" experience in their medical practices. One of my favorites was a Dr. Roskelly who, like so many attendings, regularly contributed a full day each week away from his office, to meet with M3s like us in small groups, to talk over our patients' findings and problems.

Responsibility

Once when I was on a medical service at Cook County Hospital (CCH), I hung a fresh bottle of intravenous (IV) fluids for a "brittle" diabetic patient, before I left for the night.

"Wait a minute", called the resident, "Looks like you've set that IV drip rate to last about six or seven hours. What'll happen then?"

"Um," I replied hesitantly, "The nurse or intern will hang another bottle?"

"Have you arranged that with them? We are short-staffed, and they may not have time to do your work."

"My work?"

"Sure, he's your patient. You're still responsible, even if you go home."

"What should I do?" I asked.

"Take responsibility, John. Don't ask someone else to do your work. This guy's life is in your hands: when that bottle runs dry after midnight, the IV will start sucking air, and – unless someone notices in time – your patient will die from an air embolism. Unless you want to return at midnight, why don't you hang two or three bottles interconnected? At six or more hours apiece, your guy will still be alive when you return in the morning."

I had no idea this IV interconnecting could be done, so the resident showed me how. In short-handed CCH, I guess it was the norm. Instead of standard IV poles, at CCH they used coat racks salvaged from City Hall, since each tall Oak post had half a dozen large hooks for hats and coats, and all those connected IV bottles!

I carefully checked the connections, then went home, hoping it worked properly so my patient could make it through the night. This responsibility stuff was burdensome! (Welcome to Medicine.)

And when I nervously returned in the morning, two bottles had drained, the third was still dripping nicely, and my patient was enjoying his breakfast. Whew!

Outpatients

On Outpatient Services, we were assigned daily clinic appointments with ambulatory patients. Many were new patients, some were follow-ups, and we were tasked to determine the next course of action for them. Here, we were again loosely supervised by the intern or resident physician. These clinic visits were often challenging, since patients presented at a rapid pace (perhaps every 15 minutes), all day long, with symptoms of diseases we may have never seen before, or who needed medication adjustments or refills. Every night I went home with a long list of "lookups" to read about the day's patients' conditions or medications. These early habits have proven invaluable in a career necessarily devoted to lifelong learning.

Some services expected us to perform emergency admissions and sometimes take night calls. But though it could be taxing, we were grateful for all the patient contacts we could get! On some services, such as OB-GYN, I liked to sleep in the ER, because patients came in all night, ready to deliver their babies, and I didn't want to miss assisting the intern or resident.

When sleeping in the ER, I always asked to be awakened if any kind of emergency or trauma arrived; I never wanted to sleep through an interesting or instructive case. Some diseases occurred only once per million patients, and if you missed it, you might not see it again soon. I was often reminded, "The more patients you see, the more you'll learn," and it was certainly true. I wanted to learn everything.

On the surgical services life was similar, except there were usually shorter outpatient clinic days and longer operating room (OR) days. We learned surgical hand scrubbing technique, sterile gowning, gloving, and sterile OR surgical technique. We helped the scrub nurse prep and drape the surgical site and assisted the surgeon by holding retractors (to keep the wound open, and the surgical field exposed), or by-passing instruments. Then there was record-keeping, as well as pre-op and post-op patient care. The same was true in OB-GYN: we helped the intern or resident deliver the baby, and assisted patients during labor and postpartum.

Most surgeons were even-tempered and kind, even under pressure. But others were impatient and short-tempered, especially when things got stressful. Just like bosses in any field, I supposed. I could see the value of exemplary behavior, should I ever become a boss – or a surgeon.

XXVIII

LOVING THE LEARNING

Learning Fun

It was all so magical! We dealt with front-line medical care, and got to act like "real doctors," although we were constantly aware of how much we needed to learn. But we were learning so much, almost every hour, from every patient: no matter what we were doing, we were learning something new, and it was so very thrilling for me! Some days I felt quite inadequate after missing a diagnostic clue, and occasionally I felt accomplished, after making a correct diagnosis and treatment plan all by myself!

Gold Mines

The hospitals and clinics seemed to be gold mines of information. They were filled with medical and surgical patients of all types, needing diagnoses and treatments of all kinds, along with plenty of staffers to teach us. We never stopped learning and there was always easy access to all this information and good advice.

Autopsy Lunch

At Cook County clinics, I enjoyed taking my lunch up to the pathology department, where I watched autopsies performed. Watching the diseased or damaged organs being removed, weighed, and examined, while chewing on a sandwich, might sound distasteful, but I loved it all! The pathologists always explained in detail what they were seeing and doing with the organs they were handling while dictating their findings for the record.

I was impressed when the cancerous lungs of heavy smokers were sliced open, filled with sticky black tobacco tar! I was still a cigarette smoker at the time, and realized that I had better quit pretty soon! Although habits were slow to change, it was becoming clear to us all that cigarette smoking was a very unhealthy – even dangerous – habit.

Dad showed me this photo of him when he lived at the infirmary during his residency. His pince-nez glasses were all the rage at the time.

Dad's Visit

That fall, my dad was attending the 1961 meeting of the American Academy of Ophthalmology and Otolaryngology (EENT), annually held at the Palmer House hotel in Chicago. One afternoon he stopped by the Infirmary for a sentimental visit. I knew Dad had taken his residency training in Chicago but was completely surprised to learn that he had served his EENT Residency in our IEEI building over 30 years earlier, climbing those same steps and walking in the same front door!

Dad enjoyed walking through the crowded clinics, recalling his several years working there, "Busy as ever!" he remarked. Then he came upstairs to visit my room. Now I was really stunned, as he looked around and said, "Gosh, nothing has changed up here! I probably lived in this very room of yours! In those days we residents were all single and lived in the building where we were trained." It seemed remarkable that father and son could be standing together in the same room he occupied almost 35 years ago: What an amazing happenstance! *Providential*?

I remained in Chicago over '61 Christmas, visiting my grandma Lavinia, my dad's friend Bill Burns, as well as my Uncle Steve's family in Flossmoor, and enjoyed some good imported Czech beer with Phil Miller, home for the holidays.

Spring '62

We continued our M3 clinical rotations, seeing patients by day, and studying about them every night. Jan had enough big city living and moved to Peoria, Illinois to take a better job at St. Francis Hospital, and I missed my "passionate Passavant" weekends.

Au Revoir

I escaped to Peoria on my bike for a weekend visit to Jan's apartment in the St. Francis Nurses' Quarters. We enjoyed our usual exciting reunion encounter, but the excitement just wasn't the same. I expected she might be seeing someone else, which was not surprising, and was certainly a good idea for her, since our pragmatic relationship was likely a dead end for Jan.

After my return, a strongly scented shirt box arrived for me, which the mailroom lady, Opal Beltz, joked about. Inside I found Jan's familiar little sheer nightie, doused with one of her favorite perfumes, Shalimar or Tabu. Her nightie was happily torn from our more energetic unions. The card tucked in said something like, "Thanks for the memories!" I was swept up by the perfumed nightie nostalgia, recapturing the emotions of two years of unforgettable amorous encounters! I kept the nightie under my pillow for a very long time, until the scent was gone.

Thanks, Jan, what a gift you were!

Motorcycle Therapy

On spring break I felt the urge to get out of town, so I arranged Infirmary coverage, hopped on my BMW and took a road trip alone to Florida, camping along the way in my old pup tent. I went to visit Bill Carter, my mentor from the Honolulu Kaiser Hospital ER training adventures three years before. He and his wife were in Panama City, where he had opened a Family Practice Clinic. I was really attracted to this idea of being a general practitioner, caring for patients from newborns to elderly grandmas, and everyone in between. We had a lovely couple of days together, visiting his clinic and talking about the joy of medical practice. Although I was still just a "junior doctor," it was great fun to share clinical stories with Bill. Escaping Chicago and camping along the highway was very therapeutic.

There was no summer break this year since our twenty-one-month clinical rotation calendar ran consecutively. So we continued the routine of seeing patients by day and learning about them by reading at night.

Rush Letters

During the summer Dave and I crafted a series of cleverly written and very informative med school orientation letters, to be sent from Phi Beta Pi to all 200 incoming freshmen, intended to introduce medical education and fraternities. These letters were highlighting our frat in particular, prior to Rush Week. This was a series of six very detailed letters.

The project was a lot of work! Very long hours dealing with weekly deadlines for writing, printing, folding, stuffing, addressing, and mailing 200 copies. It was a time-consuming and exhausting partnership with Dave. Finally, he became so fed up with dealing with my obsessive-compulsive deadlines and impatient demands, that he quit. He didn't argue or fight, he simply said that I was giving him an ulcer, so he just packed-up and moved out. He moved into the apartment of a fellow frat brother, and we spent our M4 year apart.

Looking back, Dave certainly took the healthy path, though it was a great sacrifice for him, missing free rent, and all the meals and laundry.

Lesson Re-learned

I couldn't blame Dave for walking out. I had created a monster-job that was really too much for two busy school guys: six letters in as many weeks, written, printed, and mailed to 200 addressees! Crazy stuff!

But I had a compulsion to make it happen, and to make it perfect: to decrease the number of letters would reduce the information shared; to recruit helpers would require hours of training and supervision. My obsessive-compulsive nature wouldn't allow me to back down, so I pushed Dave and myself too hard. I'd already forgotten the "slave driver" lesson of Work Week! After Dave left, I became both slave driver and slave, and, with some pharmaceutical help, managed to finish the job alone.

Sorry, Dave!

The informative letter series proved very popular with incoming freshmen and distinguished our fraternity, which substantially increased Phi Bete enrollment. Naturally we all showed up for Rush Week to help recruit and orient the candidates and sing the bawdy songs and limericks. And drink the beer.

Regardless of their choice of fraternity, incoming freshmen saved the letters, which provided information not available elsewhere, and I was told they were passed along for years.

The beloved Meister Brau half-gallon, mounted as a memorial tribute.

Bachelor Beer Club

A popular and inexpensive beer was Meister Brau. Every spring the brewery created a limited edition of its popular Bock Beer (a stronger, darker German beer, usually brewed in the spring for May Festivals.) This was available in half-gallon bottles, and on Saturday afternoons at the Infirmary, Dave, Bruce, and I enjoyed sitting together in our quarters, drinking our big bottles of Bock. We called it our Bock Bachelor Club. When Bock season was over, we continued the happy Saturday tradition with half-gallons of regular Meister Brau beer.

We soon named the party our "Saturday Afternoon Meister Brau Bachelor Beer Club," or SAMBBBC. In recent years we three have strived to hold periodic annual reunions of the SAMB^{3}C.

2022: John, Dave, and Bruce Reunion on the 60th anniversary of SAMB3C.

XXIX

Last Lap

Procedures

We began our final year in the fall '62 semester as M4s, continuing our assigned clinical rotations. Although the country was focused on the re-emergence of *Rock and Roller* Elvis Presley, and the frightening Cuban Missile Crisis, we paid little attention, since we were so busy and intently preoccupied by our patients and our training.

Whichever service we might be assigned, there were certain procedures common to them all: blood counts, urinalysis, venipuncture, intravenous fluid infusions, urinary catheterization, nasogastric feeding tubes, spinal taps, etc.

One day, the intern on my service came by and said, "I'm assigned to make sure you M4s know how to do all these procedures and feel comfortable with them." I replied that I had done them all more than once, except for urethral catheterization and spinal tap.

Spinal Tap

"OK," he said, "let's do a spinal." He took two of us to see a patient admitted for severe headaches whom the intern was preparing for a spinal tap: he did the sterile skin prep and drape, gave a shot of local anesthetic, and said, "Now, watch closely." Then he explained each step of the procedure. He first counted the vertebral spines, then placed the long needle through the correct inter-vertebral space, into the spinal canal. He measured the pressure, and withdrew two cc (cubic centimeters) of spinal fluid, to be sent to the lab for analysis.

"Now it's your turn," he said, leading us down the hall, while the nurse took over the patient.

We came to the room of another patient, also prepped for a spinal tap. I put on my gloves, injected the anesthetic, checked the location by counting the spines, then picked up the sterile syringe and needle, and proceeded to do my tap. I had to repeat my entry a few times before fluid appeared, and each time the intern told me what I needed to correct. He told the other M4 to check with him tomorrow when there would be another patient ready for a tap.

Bladder Tap

"Now, catheterization," he said, leading us to the men's restroom. "I've got no patients needing a cath at the moment, so just show me how you would do it."

"On myself?" I replied.

"Why not?" he said. "Then you'll know how it feels." So I dropped my pants, and he handed me an alcohol wipe and anesthetic lube. Then he produced a Foley (inflatable, retention) catheter from a sterile package, and clamped the drain line so my urine wouldn't spill out.

Like all the procedures we first performed, we had never done them before, and it was the same for this one. I had a bit of trepidation, but knew the anesthetic lube would make entry comfortable, though I wasn't sure about sliding the catheter the rest of the way up and into my bladder.

I didn't want to seem fearful for the intern. So, attempting to appear resolute, I cautiously slipped the catheter into my penis and carefully slid it up my urethra into my bladder. Although painless, it was quite a strange feeling!

"Now, inflate it," he said. I blew a syringe of air into the inflation tube to fill the retention bulb in my bladder. When the catheter is to be retained in the bladder, this bulb holds it in place, so it won't easily slip out. To finish the procedure I then deflated the bulb and withdrew the catheter.

Whew!

My partner M4 watched all this with intense interest. When I left, he had applied the lube and was cautiously inserting his own urethral catheter.

There was a maxim in the training: "See one, do one, teach one." As I left, the intern said, "Remember now, John, you've seen one and done one, so now it's your turn to teach one. Tomorrow, I'm sending you a couple M4s for you to teach how to catheterize, and maybe tap." And so, I did.

New Friend

One night at The Owl's I met a graduate nurse from Minot, North Dakota, Una B, and we soon were enjoying a lovely relationship, until she was offered a job at Henry Ford Hospital in Detroit. I thought that would be the end, but I missed our fun so much that one weekend – at her invitation – I jumped on my bike and drove to Detroit – more than 300 miles then – for a short but exciting reunion: energetic young lust!

The weather was getting cold up north, so I didn't repeat the trip, and soon it was time for Christmas break.

Thanks, Una; I loved your climactic giggles!

There were a couple other brief encounters but none so memorable as Una.

XXX

Astonishing Encounter

Final Semester

In January 1963, we began our final semester of med school. It all seemed to have happened so quickly, but we sure knew a lot more than when we arrived, though not nearly enough! During my surgical rotation I was approached by the Chief Surgical and Resident. He complimented me on my progress and offered me the opportunity to cover for one of the interns who would be leaving for his two-week vacation. As a mere M4, I'd get to "play intern" on his inpatient medical service for two weeks. I jumped at the chance, since I'd have more responsibility, and learn more in preparation for my own upcoming year as an intern.

Baby Intern

The departing intern introduced me to some of his inpatients and their cases, and I took his job the following week. Interns worked all day and spent every other night on call. Since I could not take night call while living in the Infirmary, I arranged coverage for my chart and phone duties, and I simply lived at the hospital for two weeks, usually sleeping and showering in an unoccupied room on my assigned medical floor. (Depending on their illness or condition, patients are placed on dedicated floors, such as medical, surgical, or pediatric floors.)

Red Urine

One night I was sleeping on a gurney in a supply room when the night nurse awakened me, to show me a glass of what looked just like Coca-Cola. She said, "The patient in room 213 just peed this. What would you like me to do?"

Nurses were notorious for playing tricks on new interns, and as a "pretend intern," I thought that this might be the situation. I sleepily took the glass, sniffed it, and to call her bluff, said something like, "You can't fool me! Here, I'll show you, it's just Coke," gesturing as if about to drink it.

"No, no!" she said, as she grabbed the glass back, "This is real!" Apparently, it was real, and not knowing the patient's condition, or meds, I didn't want to speculate on several causes of red-brown urine. So, I asked her to call the urology resident for instructions, then get back to me if necessary.

Small World!

Before I fell back to sleep, we had a little chat, and I learned her name was Mary Jo Stelk. She had graduated from the Presbyterian-St. Luke's School of Nursing last September. The next night she returned to tell me that she told her mom she met a nice M4 named John Corboy. Her mom asked if he was, "any relation to Phil Corboy, formerly of Valparaiso, Indiana?"

Astonished, I responded that Phil Corboy was my father, and he was raised in Valparaiso. Mary Jo relayed this to her mom, who reported that she had "Once dated Phil Corboy," when her family lived in Valparaiso, in a cottage on Flint Lake. I knew my dad was born and raised in Valparaiso and learned from Mary Jo's mom that he had taken her for a canoe ride or two, when they were high school students. What a small world!

Mary Jo bravely tries the BMW.

Spring Fun

That spring Mary Jo's parents, who were now living in Chicago, were staying in their Flint Lake cottage. Mary Jo joined them on weekends and invited me to come for a visit. I was delighted to get out of Chicago for a weekend, and the motorcycle trip to Valparaiso was less than an hour. Her parents, Jo and Harold (Hap) Stelk, were simply delightful people. My dad was happy to learn of this unlikely connection to Valparaiso, where he grew up, had a medical practice, and where I was raised, as well.

Mary Jo and I had fun boating on Flint Lake, and I convinced her to ride on the back of my motorcycle into town, where I showed her the apartment building at 207 Washington Street, where I was conceived and spent my first five years.

207 Washington, where I was conceived and spent my first five years.

Sentimental Visit

This was an emotional visit because I remembered exactly the layout of the building and our upstairs apartment. Mary Jo and I climbed the stairs, I knocked on the door of our former apartment, and said hello to the current residents. They were quite surprised when I explained, "I grew up in this apartment and left here 18 years ago in 1945, to live in Hawaii." I have a great love for that building and have been back to visit several times during the intervening decades.

I made several weekend bike trips to the Stelk's Flint Lake cottage, and on spring break even spent a couple of days there. Mary Jo and I were becoming quite close friends. She impressed me as a very special girl: smart and attractive, as many of the nurses were, but with a delightful personality – flexible, good sport, adventuresome, with a great sense of humor. I found that I really enjoyed her company!

On one of these Valparaiso spring visits, I took her to see my dad's original EENT office at 8 Monroe Street that he had opened 28 years before.

Meanwhile, Dave Cope had forgiven me for my high-pressure micro-management of our fraternity letters project, and we rekindled our friendship over our love for motorcycling. He joined me on a couple of trips to Valparaiso, along with his girlfriend Sally Scott, who happened to be Mary Jo's roommate; they'd been together all through nursing school. So, we became quite an agreeable foursome: two guy pals partying on the lake with two gal pals. We all enjoyed sleeping outdoors on the large porch swings MJ's grandad had made.

MJ and I biked to visit Dad's 1935 office.

XXXI

REAL DOCTORS?

Finality

Our clinical rotations concluded in early June, and we sat through more grueling days of National Medical Boards Part II, to determine if we were qualified to take the next academic step, which at that time was an internship. We were now qualified!

Regret

Before the graduation ceremony, formal photographs were taken of our University of Illinois MD Class of 1963. I recall that Dave and I, tired after four years of Administration's demands, foolishly boycotted the photo session, in favor of taking a bike ride in the country. In retrospect, this is one of my few regrets from those U of I days, because our photos and names were not included in our '63 Class Archives. It appears as though we never graduated!

Graduation

After seven to eight years of college and med school preparation, we graduated in June, and received our degrees as Doctors of Medicine. We were now "real" Medical Doctors, although we humbly realized that we still had a lot to learn. My new friend, Mary Jo, attended the event.

My parents flew from Hawaii for the impressive ceremony at the McCormick Convention Center Auditorium. They were so proud: their formerly troublesome teenager was doing okay, so far!

Mary Jo's beautiful graduation photo.

Graduate with MJ.; "What's this funny hat?"; Proud Mom and me.

Inspiration

I don't know whether it was part of the graduation address, but somewhere along the way I was inspired by the admonition of the great William Osler, MD:

> ***"As Physicians, our Task is***
> ***To cure sometimes,***
> ***To relieve often,***
> ***But to comfort always."***

I've tried always to practice these precepts in my medical career, and to teach them to my students.

Planning Ahead

Our country was enmeshed in the Viet Nam War, and we grads knew that we'd been deferred from military service through college and med school, and we understood that after our internship, most of us would immediately be drafted to serve as military doctors. We talked of paying special attention to management of major ("battlefield-type") trauma cases during our coming internships.

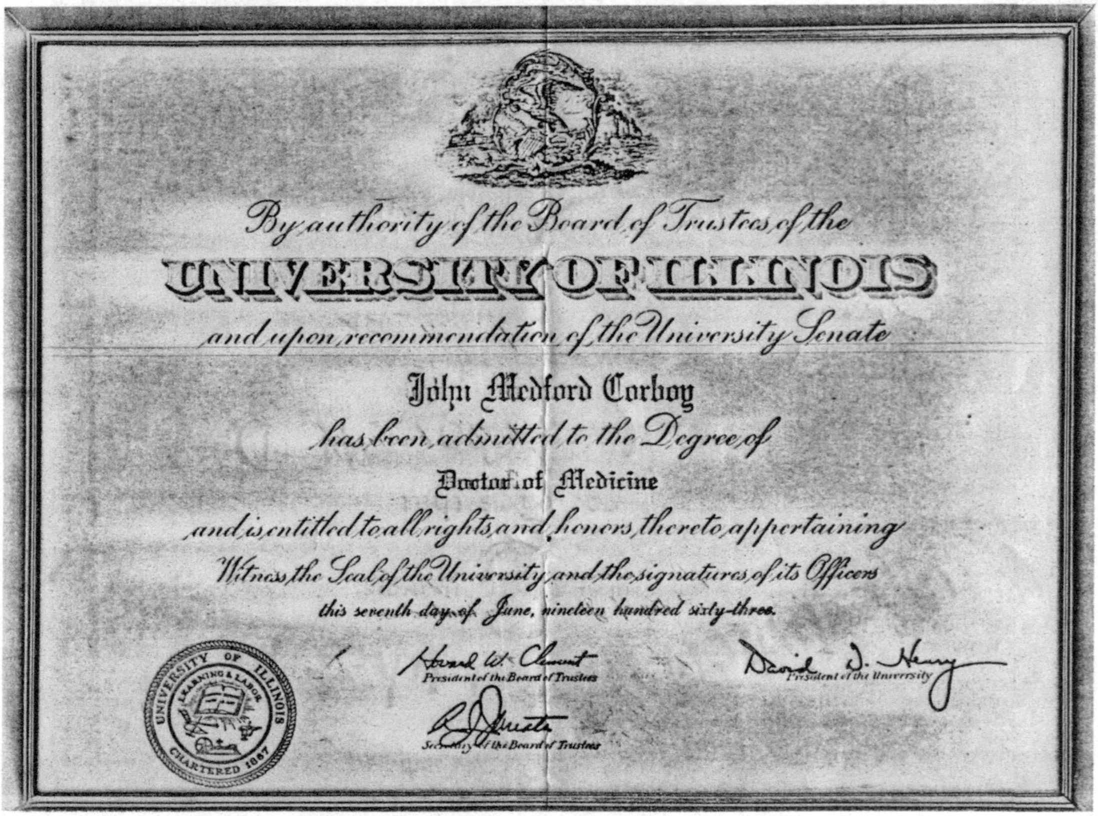

By authority of the Board of Trustees of the

UNIVERSITY OF ILLINOIS

and upon recommendation of the University Senate

John Medford Corboy

has been admitted to the Degree of

Doctor of Medicine

and is entitled to all rights and honors thereto appertaining

Witness the Seal of the University and the signatures of its Officers

this seventh day of June, nineteen hundred sixty-three.

President of the Board of Trustees

President of the University

Secretary of the Board of Trustees

UNIVERSITY OF ILLINOIS

LEARNING & LABOR

CHARTERED 1867

My diploma.

Part 3

Internship/ Wedding

XXXII

PSLH INTERNSHIP

Busy Rewarding Life

I had been accepted for '63-'64 at Presbyterian (now Rush)-St. Luke's Hospital (PSLH) as a Rotating Intern, since I was attracted to family practice. As proof of our rank, we now donned the long white coat, and received a salary: $150 per month, my first medical paycheck.

Internships were classified as Rotating, for those like me who wanted to do general practice, and wanted "more of everything," or those who were unsure of a specialty interest, so they could experience a broad range of medical disciplines. Whereas Straight Internships were for those who had already chosen a specialty for their coming residency training, such as straight pediatric, straight surgical, or straight OB-GYN, etc.

Internship Goal

The Internship's objective was for us to manage patients just as we would in our future medical practices. There would be minimal, but ever-present, supervision, simply to confirm that we were managing patients correctly. For those of us in a Rotating Internship, heading for a community family or general practice, this was our last opportunity in a training center to see and do and learn as much as humanly possible.

Housing

PSLH owned the nearby Kidston House, an apartment building where its single nurses and nursing students lived, and several floors were reserved for PSLH interns and residents.

Immediately after graduation, I said goodbye to all at the Infirmary – and was quickly replaced by an eager Phi Bete M3 – and moved into Kidston. My assigned roommate was Steve Ruskin, who was doing a straight OB-GYN Internship. We began our assigned clinical responsibilities promptly on July 1.

As a rotator, I spent two months each on Pediatrics (where Mary Jo now worked), and OB-GYN (where I assisted with or delivered more than 100 babies). Then followed four months on Internal Medicine, including psychiatry and dermatology. A final four months on Surgery completed the rotation, during which I could choose elective sub-specialties, so along with general surgery (thinking of battlefield trauma), I selected those I thought would be most useful to a family practice: urology, orthopedics, and ear, nose, and throat.

My pal Dave Cope chose his internship at St. Francis Hospital in Peoria because it had a very strong, personalized educational program. I was sorry to lose Dave's companionship, but we planned to request the same dates for our vacations, the next spring, to ride our bikes on a camping trip down the Mississippi River.

Working Hours

Our internship schedule was rather strenuous: we were expected to be "On 36, off 12," for each 48-hour cycle. This meant we were to be available for all the "36 on" hours, so I usually slept in the hospital or the ER, just to keep close and not miss anything. I usually went home only during my "12 off" shift.

Our "36 On" hours were spent seeing patients by day in the hospital or clinics, the operating room (OR), or in the labor/delivery room (L&D). Each night we were to be available on a moment's notice for night and emergency calls, which is why I napped in the ER on a gurney. Many of us soon learned, as soldiers do, how to quickly fall asleep anytime, anywhere, and that useful habit has served me well throughout my life.

Food "Service"

As interns, we could receive free meals at the hospital cafeteria, but we seldom had time to sit for meals; we usually preferred to snack from the patients' abandoned meal trays. For example, if the patients were discharged early, before their lunch tray arrived, we'd help ourselves to the untouched meal. Similarly, if their lunch was served at noon, but they arrived late at four, we would enjoy picking from the bedside tray. As M4s we had also liked to do this, but only after the higher-ranking interns had helped themselves.

Our "12 Off" hours allowed a welcome return to our quarters for a shower and rest in a real bed, and maybe time for a decent cafeteria meal. Then we were back on duty, to begin the next 48-hour cycle. Sometimes we had Sunday off, but oftentimes not.

"Ouch!"

Sometimes after unusually busy nights without much sleep, then assisting the surgeon in the OR the following day, I would fight to stay awake while standing motionless and silent holding a retractor, especially after lunch. As I drifted off, the wound I was holding open would slowly close, when the surgeon's wordless, sharp crack on my knuckles with an instrument would snap me awake!

Beepers

We interns received "beepers," which were quite an intern/resident status symbol, but at the time these "high-tech" devices simply signaled us to respond to the hospital telephone operator, who relayed our message. We were to keep these turned on, and carried on our person, during our entire "36 on" shift.

XXXIII

NATIONAL TRAGEDY

Always Learning

We never complained about the hours, since we were learning something new every minute, and wasn't that the whole point? "You snooze, you lose." I rarely saw my roommate Steve since his call schedule didn't match mine. If it weren't for our rumpled beds and some trash in the wastebasket, neither of us would have been aware we had a roommate.

National Tragedy

I vividly recall a particular Friday morning, November 22, a week before Thanksgiving, as I reviewed my patients' x-rays with the radiologist. Suddenly the venerable voice of veteran CBS television broadcaster Walter Cronkite burst over the hospital speaker system, solemnly announcing the assassination of U.S. 35th President John F. Kennedy in Dallas, Texas. There was stunned silence in the room. It seemed inconceivable: he was so young and popular, how could something like this happen? The silence was eventually broken by the radiologist: "C'mon, let's finish these films!"

The story, with its now well-known major players, soon unfolded. But it was many months before the nation collectively gathered its emotions following this unthinkable national tragedy. The conspiracy stories and books soon followed.

During the Christmas holidays, Phil Miller came home to visit his family, and we concluded our plans for taking a spring motorcycle camping trip with Dave Cope down the Mississippi. I requested my vacation time to coincide with Phil's grad school spring break and Dave requested his internship vacation to coincide as well. "Formal Phil" was becoming one of the guys, and a "biker dude" at that: he'd bought a Triumph TR6 and was eager to hit the open road in the spring.

After Christmas, we resumed the rotation schedule. (There was no actual "Christmas break," since illness never takes a holiday, although elective admissions were restricted to allow staff a little family time off.)

New Bike IV

One of the benefits of an internship was that we received a salary, my first full-time paycheck since my college summer in the Foremost Dairy. We interns received $150 monthly but had virtually no time to spend it. I used my income to purchase a new motorcycle, a '63 Triumph Bonneville, a fast, dual-carbureted 650 cc powerhouse. As I recall, it cost $1500, which was ten of my monthly paychecks, plus another for tax. With my final paycheck I had a small trailer made for towing the bike behind a car.

I truly loved my "Bonnie," and the first chance I had, I rode to Valparaiso to show it off, only to find that the Stelk family was in Chicago that weekend. I treasured it so much that I dragged it onto the cottage porch for safe keeping while I slept overnight.

When I had a rare Sunday off, I loved taking a sunrise ride along Lake Shore Drive. My '63 white Bonneville had a windshield and saddlebags; these white Bonnies were known to be "the hottest bikes on the road"; and they really were!

My new Triumph Bonneville.

HISTORICAL NOTE

"Residents" and "Fellows": Although specialty trainees no longer reside in their training institutions, they are still formally called "residents." After three to five years training as specialists, they may take additional years of sub-specialty training called fellowships. Residency and fellowship can consume up to six years or more.

XXXIV

Changing Times

Mop Tops

The single PSLH nurses lived in our same Kidston Hall, so Mary Jo came down to my apartment for occasional suppers. In February, we watched the Ed Sullivan show, featuring the debut of the new "mop top" British singers, The Beatles. What great musical entertainment! Looking back, their so-called "long hair" was not so long at all, but at the time it sure seemed that way! (Truly long-haired hippies were yet to come.)

Food Adventures

All my income was going towards motorcycle payments, so for occasional dinners at home, I looked into low-cost foods at a nearby Hispanic grocer. I became fascinated by the inexpensive organ meats available, such as "tripe" (stomach lining), and "sweet-

Happy couple at Kidston supper.

MJ checking out Christmas party dress.

bread" (thymus and pancreas). MJ was easy-going and adventuresome, so one night we enjoyed baked kidneys. She was such a good sport that another night, we dined on baked "Rocky Mountain Oysters" (bull testicles): "Tasty Testes." Not bad at all!

"The Pill"

1963 was the year of the birth control pill (BCP) arrival, and by the following spring of '64, many young women were "on the pill." (As I anticipated, this ability to prevent unwanted pregnancy led to a seismic shift in our moral culture.) There were some medical side effects of the early formulations, so we needed to request this info in our medication history. I recall that young women were often reluctant to disclose this information, lest it imply that they had a sex life. "No, no," they'd insist, "The pill is only to regulate my irregular menstrual periods."

Our popular Histology Instructor, young Graduate Student Vincent DeFeo, scoffed at the need for medical students to await political approval. Risking his doctorate, he reserved a classroom at 5pm, after official class hours, bravely gave optional, well-attended lectures on Oral Birth Control: the revolutionary concept of preventing ovulation (and menstruation) by oral hormonal control.

The controversy later evaporated (the pill was simply too popular), the subject became part of the Gynecology Curriculum, DeFeo received his Ph.D., and we all admired Dr. DeFeo for his fortitude. Thanks, Vince!

Despite the long hours, I was really enjoying my rotations, particularly the surgical subspecialties: ear, nose, and throat (ENT), urology, and orthopedics. I really learned so much about each subject that I knew would be of value in a family medical practice.

HISTORICAL NOTE

Pill Controversy: In late '62, medical information was provided to the profession in advance of the pill's national release the following spring.

So controversial was the morality of this concept of pregnancy prevention with a simple pill, that our med school could not actually teach about the endocrine physiology (preventing ovulation) to medical students without approval of the Board of Trustees of the University of Illinois. The trustees were, in turn, said to be concerned with the reaction of the Catholic Church to artificial birth control.

XXXV

GREAT RIVER RIDE

Dave's Disaster

Soon it was vacation time and Phil Miller showed up on his new Triumph TR6 to join me on the trip to Peoria to pick up Dave Cope. When we arrived, we were stunned: Dave was hospitalized! A couple of days before, Dave had been in a very serious accident on his motorcycle, when he rear-ended a parked car. His bike crashed under the car, and he flew over it, landing on the hood, where the hood ornament shredded his helmet. Broke several bones and ripped a hip apart!

We met Dave in the hospital, where he was full of IVs, covered with plaster casts, and strung-up in traction. The poor guy was really injured! The shattered helmet had probably saved his life. It was clear Dave would not be traveling for many months, and in fact had to repeat a portion of his internship due to his medical absence.

Phil and I enjoyed our riverside camping trip, following The Great River Road, a scenic highway that regularly crossed the Mississippi from one side to the other. We had time for a brief hotel stay in New Orleans and enjoyed Bourbon Street, the French Quarter, street jazz, and the usual "Big Easy" revelry. Then we sped quickly up the river and back to work.

XXXVI

JAILBIRD

Under the Influence

I spent a rare Sunday off with Mary Jo and some friends partying at the Flint Lake cottage, and we all had great fun with boating and beer. My pal Marty Schafer (heading for a Cardiology Residency), joined the fun to show us his hot new Plymouth Judge sedan, renowned for its astonishing acceleration. He invited some of our friends to hop in, then let me drive it on the nearby forest roads. We came out of the woods at an intersection, where I stopped for the red light.

When the light turned green, I hit the accelerator too hard, and with tires squealing, the car rocketed ahead, fishtailing wildly across the intersection and sideswiped an approaching car! Clearly, I underestimated the amazing acceleration, and reacted too slowly, because of all the beer. The police arrived, and I was cited for "heedless and careless" driving and fined something like $35. I didn't have the cash, nor did the pals in the car, so I was jailed until I could raise the money.

There was minor damage to both cars, but major damage to my ego! Marty drove the group back to the cottage where they took up a collection among the others.

Meanwhile, I sat in a jail cell for several hours, along with two other miscreants. Soon it was Sunday evening, and a local minister and his wife brought us a lovely hot dinner of cornbread, pork, and beans. I was clear-headed and hungry by now and was so grateful to receive this delicious home-cooked meal. Despite this kindness, these two jerks were rude and muttered mean and insulting remarks to the sweet church lady, which I felt was despicable! I did my best to show her our gratitude.

Captivity

My friends let me "stew" for a while, then later returned with the money they collected, and I was soon released. Interestingly, nothing was ever said about my driving "under the influence." I later arranged to reimburse the kids, pay repair and insurance costs for both vehicles, and the incident was soon forgotten.

But I never forgot the frightening feeling of being locked up, and at the mercy of a jailer. I thought the worst thing about the situation was my captivity; my loss of freedom. My heedless cellmates thought the worst thing about jail was the quality of the free food. They didn't seem to mind the captivity, so long as they had "three hots and a cot."

XXXVII

Draft Notice

Drafted!

In January, I received a curious Selective Service Notice of my appointment to the Commission Corps of the US Public Health Service (USPHS), Department of Health, Education, and Welfare (DHEW), to the rank of Assistant Surgeon. (I later learned it was equivalent to a Navy Lieutenant, O-3.) I had no idea why I was appointed to the PHS.

In mid-spring, I received the anticipated but cryptic notice of conscription (Military Orders). I was to "Report 7/1/64 to the MOC of the MBAH of the DFQ of the USPHS, El Paso, Texas." Well, I knew it was something about El Paso, and it wasn't the Army, Navy, or Air Force. And I was relieved that it didn't sound like Viet Nam.

Viet Nam Conflict

We had been so preoccupied with learning medicine that I hadn't read a newspaper or seen television news for several years, and I had little knowledge of political affairs. All I knew of Viet Nam was that the conflict began as a civil war when the Communist North, headquartered in Hanoi, invaded the Capitalist South, based in Saigon.

HISTORICAL NOTE

Our country had sent troops to assist the South, persuaded by the "Domino Theory," where one Asian nation after another could fall to the Chinese Communists. We had protected South Korea from the Communist North in 1950, and in 1955 we had begun doing the same in Viet Nam. In both countries the Chinese Communists were arming and funding the bellicose North. The fighting and dying in Viet Nam had been escalating for almost a decade, to increasing public opposition.

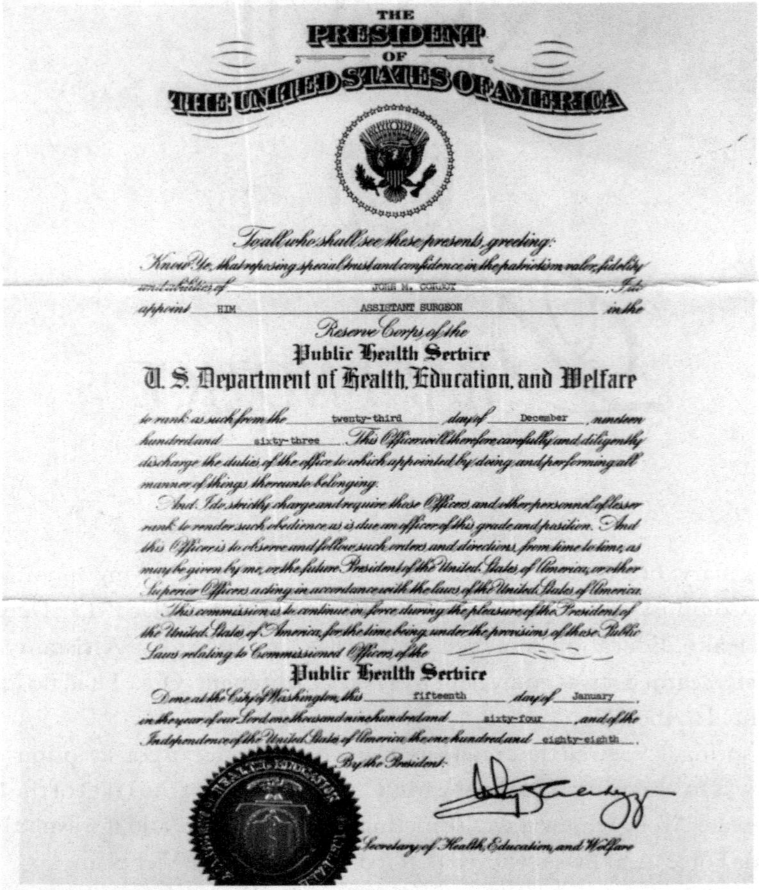

THE
PRESIDENT
OF
THE UNITED STATES OF AMERICA

To all who shall see these presents, greeting:

Know Ye, that reposing special trust and confidence in the patriotism, valor, fidelity and abilities of JOHN M. [illegible], I do appoint HIM ASSISTANT SURGEON in the

Reserve Corps of the
Public Health Service
U. S. Department of Health, Education, and Welfare

to rank as such from the twenty-third day of December, nineteen hundred and sixty-three. This Officer will therefore carefully and diligently discharge the duties of the office to which appointed by doing and performing all manner of things thereunto belonging.

And I do strictly charge and require those Officers and other personnel of lesser rank to render such obedience as is due an officer of this grade and position. And this Officer is to observe and follow such orders and directions, from time to time, as may be given by me, or the future President of the United States of America, or other Superior Officers acting in accordance with the laws of the United States of America.

This commission is to continue in force during the pleasure of the President of the United States of America, for the time being, under the provisions of those Public Laws relating to Commissioned Officers of the

Public Health Service

Done at the City of Washington, this fifteenth day of January, in the year of our Lord one thousand nine hundred and sixty-four, and of the Independence of the United States of America the one hundred and eighty-eighth.

By the President:

Secretary of Health, Education, and Welfare

My Draft Notice.

I don't believe we thought much more about it. And as medical staff, our role was not to fight – or even to understand the issues – our role was to care for our wounded troops: an obligation and an honor.

My relief in not being sent to Viet Nam was not so much to avoid the unlikely but ever-present danger, but simply to avoid the inconvenience of leaving home, country, and Mary Jo at this time.

Soon, I was able to translate the acronym-filled orders into English: I was to "Report to the Medical Officer in Charge (MOC), of the Mexican Border Area Headquarters (MBAH), of the Division of Foreign Quarantine (DFQ), of the US Public Health Service (PHS), in El Paso, Texas."

Foreign Quarantine?

This sure was surprising, but I assumed that I would learn everything when I showed up for orientation July 1, to meet the MOC of the MBAH, etc.

XXXVIII

Love Blooms

Engaged

My relationship with Mary Jo had blossomed through the spring. Our pals Dave and Sally had been married the past June after graduation. MJ and I were thinking of a future together. I loved this girl: We got along just fine, had lots of fun together, and were both flexible people. She was smart and sweet, a truly lovable girl, and I felt her pediatric skills would make her an ideal mother. She had a lovely, and loving, family, and we shared the same values, hopes and dreams. Since it was clear from my military orders that I would not be going off to war, I proposed, she accepted, and we became engaged that spring. We planned our wedding date for mid-June so that we could pack up and get to El Paso by the July 1 duty date. All very practical.

Providence

And to think this all started over a glass of urine! That's Providence, for sure!

Busy June

My internship responsibilities continued through June, until the new interns took over on July 1. We planned to drive to Texas in MJ's cute Triumph Spitfire convertible, trailering my motorcycle. But for some long-forgotten reason, we changed the plan, and I sold both the bike and trailer.

MJ and I made wedding plans, chose costumes, flowers, and attendants; we invited guests, picked wedding and reception venues, organized the reception, etc.

MCAT III

We interns took the final challenging National Board exam, Part III. The exam was a stressful annoyance amid busy June activities, but I was glad to get it out of the way. I learned in July that I passed and had become a Diplomate of the National Board of

Medical Examiners. Pretty fancy, but simply certifying that I was qualified to practice medicine.

To practice legally, I would still have to pass another exam for State Licensure, in whichever state(s) I chose to practice.

Most of my friends were drafted into one of the military services. Those that were not drafted returned for three to five additional years in Residency Training and were often called to serve afterward.

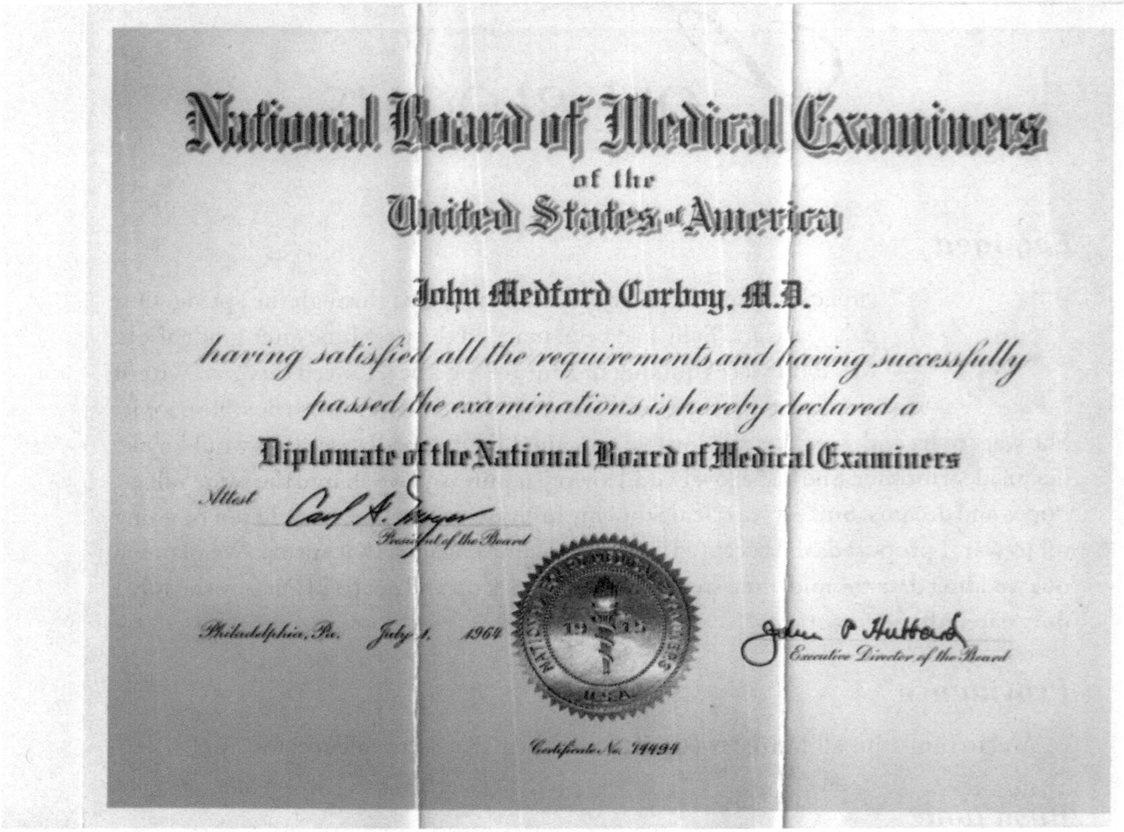

National Board of Medical Examiners
of the
United States of America

John Medford Corboy, M.D.

having satisfied all the requirements and having successfully passed the examinations is hereby declared a

Diplomate of the National Board of Medical Examiners

Attest

President of the Board

Philadelphia, Pa. July 1, 1964

Executive Director of the Board

Certificate No. 14494

The result of my eight years of grueling study and examination.

XXXIX

Wedding Bells

Our Wedding

Mary Jo and I were wed Saturday, June 27, 1964. I had five good friends as groomsmen, dressed up in fancy formal wear, with vests and Ascot ties. I remember it was a cruelly hot and humid day, and we were all miserable in our "monkey suits."

My parents attended the wedding, which was held in a Catholic Church for their benefit. As an Episcopalian, Mary Jo was required to take instruction from the priest in advance, pledging to raise any children as good little Catholics. (I never held her to this, thinking Episcopalian was just fine. Furthermore, I would never put my boys through the Catholic teen guilt cycles so troubling to my own pubescence.)

Attendants

My best pal Dave Cope could not serve as Best Man, since he had just been released from the hospital following his injuries. But at the last minute, he and his wife Sally were able to make it to the wedding, where Dave danced on crutches with his bride at the reception.

For Best Man, I chose Dave Roseman, MD, a wonderful classmate and fellow PSLH intern whom I deeply admired, who was heading for a Surgical Residency. Mary Jo chose Dave's wife Joanie as her Matron of Honor. Being Jewish, Dave was excused from some of the ritual kneeling, crossing, and praying of the Catholic Matrimonial Service. My other attendants were my Kidston roommate, Steve Ruskin, MD, future Obstetrician-Gynecologist; Phil Miller, my Experiment buddy and fellow motorcycle adventurer; college pal Marty Shafer, MD, heading for a Cardiology Residency; and fellow PSLH intern Grady Sellards, MD, future Urologist.

The wedding was followed by a lovely reception at the Olympia Fields Country Club, where I had coincidentally been a busboy eight years ago! My dad had a nice visit with MJ's mom, Jo Beals Stelk, and they talked about their small world - canoe dates of several decades ago!

Bride and Groom

Roasting in formal wear.

With my parents

Bride's parents

I love these treasured pals. L to R: Phil Miller, Best Man Dave Roseman, Grady Sellards, Steve Ruskin, Marty Shafer.

Maids and Matron of Honor with Bride.

Dave dancing with wife Sally on his crutches!

D-4 THE SUNDAY STAR-BULLETIN & ADVERTISER July 19, 1964

Miss Stelk Weds Dr. John Corboy

Mary Jo Stelk and Dr. John M. Corboy were married June 27 at St. Killians Catholic Church in Chicago.

Parents of the bride are Mr. and Mrs. Harold Stelk of Chicago, and Dr. Corboy is the son of Dr. and Mrs. Philip M. Corboy of Honolulu.

* * *

GIVEN IN marriage by her father, the bride wore a floor length gown of white organza, a matching veil of illusion and carried a cluster of lilies of the valley.

Mrs. David Roseman, the matron of honor, wore a long white taffeta gown and carried vanda orchids. Her husband, Dr. Roseman, served as best man.

For her daughter's wedding, Mrs. Stelk chose a blue lace dress with matching hat and veil and an orchid corsage. Mrs. Corboy wore a dress of yellow chiffon with a tiered hat of yellow tulle. Her corsage was of yellow orchids.

* * *

A RECEPTION was given by Mr. and Mrs. Stelk at the Olympia Fields Country Club after the ceremony. A Hawaiian trio played Island music and young Dr. and Mrs. Corboy exchanged white carnation leis at the reception. Orchids sent from Hawaii by Mr. and Mrs. Ron White of Honolulu decorated the reception area.

After a motor trip to California the young couple will be at home at 441 Orange Ave., No. 5, Coronado, Calif.

Dr. Corboy will be stationed in San Diego for two years and will enter public health service there.

* * *

MRS. CORBOY was educated at the University of Illinois and Presbyterian St. Luke's Hospital School of Nursing. She was pediatric nurse at the same hospital.

Dr. Corboy attended Punahou School and St. Louis High School and studied at Loyola University and the University of Illinois College of Medicine in Chicago.

Honolulu article the following month; sounds like a fashion review.
- Courtesy of Honolulu Star-Advertiser Archives

Tossing the garter.

Everything we own is on or in the Spitfire.

Away We Go!

Following the reception, MJ and I spent our wedding night at a hotel and the next morning we packed up her little Triumph Spitfire English sports car convertible. With traditional tin cans tied by friends to the rear bumper jangling behind us, we headed toward our future and – in just three days – our appointment with the *unknown* in El Paso.

Very proud of my successful years here in Chicago, with such great staff and colleagues.

Away we go, into our future.

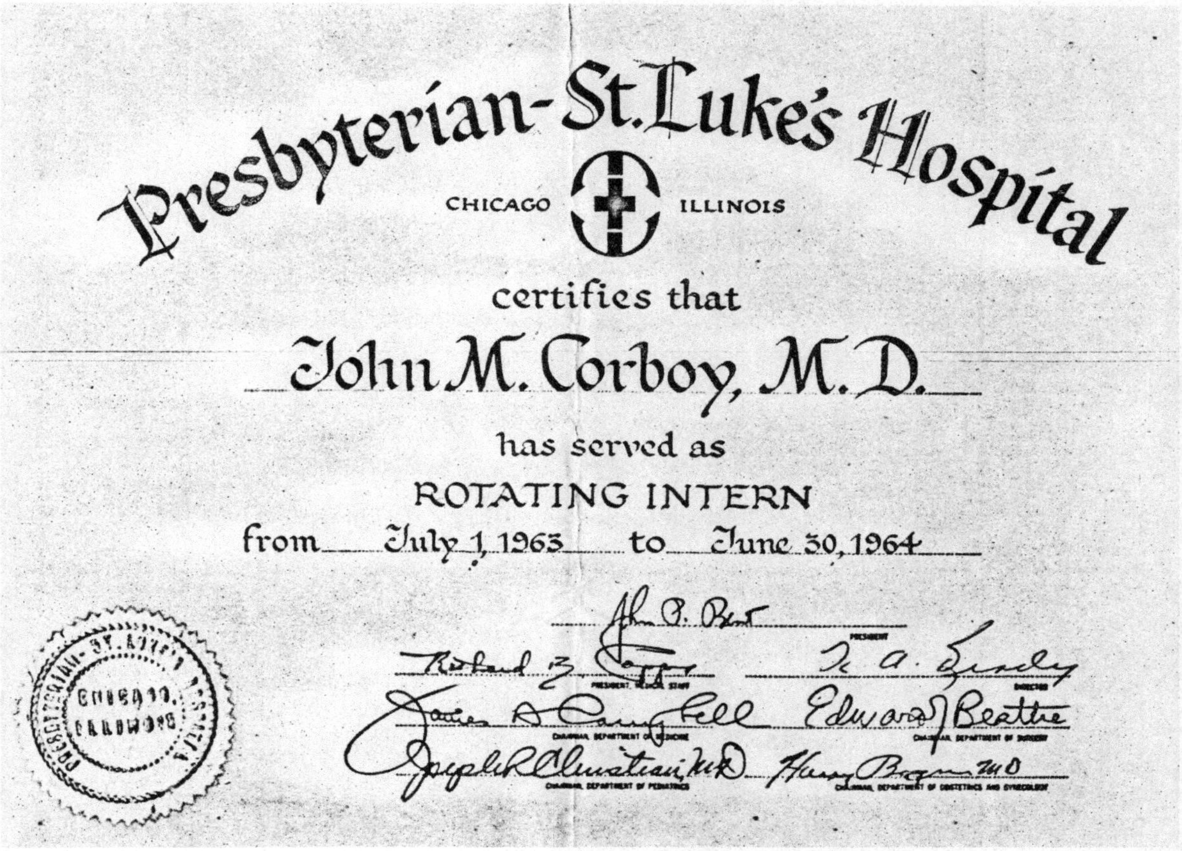

Presbyterian-St. Luke's Hospital

CHICAGO ILLINOIS

certifies that

John M. Corboy, M.D.

has served as

ROTATING INTERN

from July 1, 1963 to June 30, 1964

PRESIDENT

PRESIDENT, MEDICAL STAFF

DIRECTOR

CHAIRMAN, DEPARTMENT OF MEDICINE

CHAIRMAN, DEPARTMENT OF SURGERY

CHAIRMAN, DEPARTMENT OF PEDIATRICS

CHAIRMAN, DEPARTMENT OF OBSTETRICS AND GYNECOLOGY

This was a truly valuable experience in so many ways.

Part 4

US Public Health Service

XL

Here We Come

Honeymoon

We had a fun but strenuous three-day, 1500 mile "honeymoon" trip in MJ's '62 *Spitfire* Covertible, tent camping along the way. I had installed a luggage rack on the trunk lid, which was overloaded with all our earthly belongings.

Not much room for all our possessions in the spitfire.

Thievery

I divided the 1500 miles into three driving days of about 500 miles each. We awoke on our first morning in a lovely park to find our food gone and our campsite trashed. Neighboring campers told us this was the handiwork of the local raccoons. They kindly gave us a rope for our use the following night.

We replenished our food supplies the following day, and that night we put our food in a bag and hung it with the rope from a tree limb. We found our breakfast safe the following morning, then made the final, exhausting 500 mile run to our hotel El Paso.

Orientation

I reported for duty Wednesday, July 1, to the USPHS Mexican Border Area Headquarters (MBAH) to meet the Medical Officer in Charge (MOC), Bernard Rosenblum, MD, a high-ranking PHS Commissioned Officer. There were five of us draftees just out of internship, relieved that we were not sent off to war, but wondering about our good fortune in being assigned to serve within the United States.

Dr. Rosenblum provided three days of orientation to border quarantine policies and procedures, including a book of *U.S. Quarantine Regulations*. As Commissioned Officers (O3), we were fitted for khaki (summer) uniforms, received Uniformed Service ID cards for ourselves and Dependents (very similar to military IDs), learned military protocol, warrant *vs* commissioned officers (e.g. commissioned officers outrank warrant officers and enlisted men), etiquette and dress, saluting, and recognizing symbols of rank on uniforms of the other military services.

We learned that the US Public Health Service is one of the *seven uniformed services*, but is not an *armed service*. Nevertheless, service with the USPHS fulfilled our two-year Selective Service obligation.

Rosenblum explained that the US Public Health Service is responsible for healthcare of US Merchant Marine, US Coast Guard, Federal prisoners, Indian Health Service (including Eskimos), as well as Border Quarantine.

As Medical Officer in Charge of the Mexican Border Area Headquarters, Dr. Rosenblum oversaw five border quarantine stations: Brownsville, Eagle Pass, Juarez, Nogales, and San Ysidro. Each of us was assigned to manage medical and quarantine issues at one of the five, for the next two years, to fulfill our service obligation. Quarantine regulations and our specific medical duties at our station would be detailed by our Station Chief upon our arrival.

Rosenblum then assigned us to our duty stations. When Corboy was posted to San Ysidro, all the guys looked at me with pity: *poor guy!* Since no one had ever heard of San Ysidro, they assumed it was some God-forsaken desert outpost.

My Good Fortune

The final Friday afternoon, as the rest of the guys left to head for their duty stations, Rosenblum took me aside to explain about San Ysidro.

He said, "I understand you had requested the Coast Guard at your induction physical in high school. Unlike the other Armed Forces who have their own Medical Departments, the Coast Guard's medical services have been provided by the USPHS since 1798. Since you are now a physician, you can serve in the Coast Guard as a PHS Physician. I am assigning you to the Coast Guard Air Station (CGAS) Outpatient Clinic in San Diego, where you will begin your duties in a week."

"However," he went on, "that clinic is only half days, so the other half-days I'm assigning you to our Quarantine Station on the border at San Ysidro. The CGAS Clinic may be closing in the near future, to merge with the Balboa Naval Hospital Outpatient Clinic, and when that happens you will be full-time Deputy MOC of the San Ysidro

Quarantine Station."

Pointing to the large border wall-map, he said,"It's the one right here, on the California border with Tijuana, just south of San Diego. It's a really nice post."

Yahoo! Suddenly I became very excited: to be on the ocean in San Diego and at the Tijuana border as well, just sounded so amazing!

Providence?

I'd almost forgotten that I had requested the Coast Guard when I was a high school senior, in loving hopes of catching up with Shirley Rollinson. And this forgotten romance had resulted in the best possible border station for my military service! Certainly, more *Providence!*

XLI

New Home

Coronado

Mary Jo and I drove to San Diego, stopping briefly to visit friends working at the spectacular Carlsbad Caverns. They gave us a private tour. She thought San Diego seemed "too big and busy," which seemed odd from a Chicago native, but she'd had enough of the big city, perhaps seeking serenity. Friends had suggested we visit Coronado, a small town on the Bay across from San Diego. They said this is an island-like community beside North Island Naval Air Station (NASNI), atop a peninsula connected to the South by the *Silver Strand*. This scenic oceanside highway separates San Diego Bay and the Pacific Ocean.

We were told that Coronado was quiet and had little traffic because it's like an island,

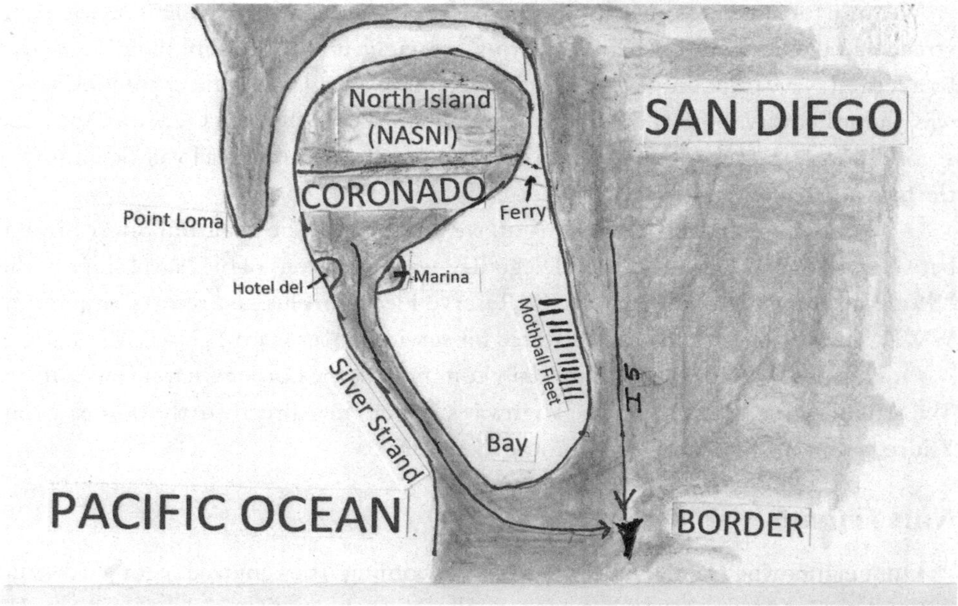

My drawing of Coronado atop San Diego Bay.

First home of our marriage.

isolated from San Diego by the Bay, and crossing to Coronado required a car-ferry ride. (A beautiful but initially controversial bridge from San Diego to Coronado, replaced the ferry in 1969.)

We took the fun 20-minute ferry trip, then drove down Orange Avenue, the main street. Mary Jo loved the look and feel of the quiet island community, so we chose a little cafe, bought a newspaper, and read the apartment rental ads.

We were fortunate to find a lovely one-bedroom, furnished apartment on the main street, at 441 Orange Ave. This was a two-story, eight-unit apartment building owned by a retired Navy Captain. The other seven tenants were all Navy officer couples. There was a large laundry room and a place to park our Spitfire in the rear. Ours was Apt 5, the second-floor, street-front apartment, the best one of all! This was a lovely location for the first home of our marriage.

After moving our few possessions in, we drove down the beautiful Silver Strand, between the Pacific Ocean and San Diego Bay, with its dozens of big Naval ships of the "Mothball Fleet" (officially the Pacific Reserve Fleet, surplus and reserve ships from WWII, some of which had been activated for service in Viet Nam.)

Our purpose was to check out my daily commute to the border Quarantine Station. The Strand merged with Interstate Highway 5, which runs directly to the border at San Ysidro, a very convenient twenty-minute scenic drive.

New Friends

Our neighboring Navy couples were very welcoming. They enjoyed regular weekend cocktail gatherings, so we soon met them all. They told me that with our military ID cards, we'd have access to all the base facilities at nearby North Island Naval Air Station, including Navy Exchange (general merchandise), Commissary (groceries), package liquor store, barber shop, and in uniform, even the Admiral Kidd Officers Club.

My khaki unform matched the Navy's, except for the collar and cap Insignia.I was reminded that in the uniform of a Naval Officer, I must carefully follow protocol, being sure to recognize from a distance who I should salute, and who I could expect to salute me. My shoulder boards indicated my rank of full Lieutenant (Navy, O3). They said at that rank I'd mostly be the recipient of salutes, which are *always* returned. Things were sounding better and better!

Quarantine Station

Once we were settled, I drove to the border and found the Quarantine Station, my first job as a physician! I was met by Paul Purlia, the Station Chief and Ana Maldonado, the bilingual administrative secretary. The staff of sixteen inspectors worked at the border station, airport and harbor, screening human and cargo arrivals. At these locations, there were four Agencies screening: Customs, Immigration, Agriculture, and Public Health.

Mr. Purlia told me I'd be Deputy MOC to Dr. T. Carey Barr, the MOC. I'd have a government car and I'd learn more about the border inspection system soon enough. I'd be examining border crossers for various excludable conditions, and reading 300 mini X-Rays each day. For now, he said, I should report tomorrow morning at the Coast Guard Air Station (CGAS) Outpatient Clinic because this border station would be my afternoon job.

Coast Guard Clinic

First thing the next morning I found the US Coast Guard Air Station Outpatient Clinic, near the San Diego Lindbergh Field Airport. I met the lead Medical Corpsman, Master Chief Ramos, who welcomed and oriented me, explaining that I'd see a morning-full of outpatients daily; active-duty young men, their wives, and some children.

I felt pretty confident handling these patients, although I'd occasionally confront a tropical skin disorder or something with which I was unfamiliar, and I would ask Chief Ramos for help. He would discreetly define the condition and its usual treatment. Now and then, I could teach him something, but I *always*

So proud to be in my new uniform.

One afternoon reading X-rays in my new office.

learned something from his thirty-five years of medical experience.

We enjoyed a rewarding partnership: although I was his superior officer, I was smart and humble enough to always ask his experienced opinion when I was uncertain, just as I would have asked faculty members at med school. When necessary, I was always able to easily refer my patients needing further evaluation or treatment to the nearby Balboa Naval Hospital.

Border Orientation

That afternoon, Mary Jo drove with me down to the border, so that I could return home in my assigned government car. Mr. Purlia gave me the keys and a government credit card for gas and repairs. It was pretty impressive to have this for my use. The car was labeled on both sides *US Government Property for Official Use Only*. I asked Purlia if it was acceptable to use this for my daily commute. He said that, as Deputy MOC, I was on quarantine call at the border, the airport and the harbor, plus two desert sub-stations *at all times*, as well as the Coast Guard Clinic. Since I needed to keep the car handy, it would be perfectly acceptable that my use was necessary for *official business*.

Mary Jo was thankful to have her car back to commute to San Diego. She quickly found a Registered Nurse position in the San Diego Health Center, secured her California RN license, and began managing the Pediatric Clinic, dealing with immunizations, well-baby exams, maternal instruction, etc. She commuted to and from her work every day by ferry.

New Duties

At the border I was introduced to Dr. Barr, who'd been away on leave. He had been

Deputy for a year and was now the MOC, so I became his Deputy. In my office I had an X-ray reading device where I'd review those 300 mini-films our inspectors took every day. Those applicants whose films showed evidence of tuberculosis or other communicable lung disorders, were held back. They were told to return to Tijuana and get a full-size chest X-ray for my evaluation.

I also performed physicals on crossing applicants: men for venereal and other diseases (por favor bajase los pantalones Señor) and on women for the same, as well as pregnancy (Señora, esta usted embarazada?). Our policy was to restrict pregnant women from entering the country, lest their newborns become automatic US citizens, "anchor babies", who then could invite their parents and dozens of relatives to join them in the United States. There was a manual of restricted conditions, such as serious mental disorders, contagious or infectious diseases, etc. My inspectors strictly enforced these policies intended to protect American citizens. Ms. Maldonado, Rod Rodriguez, or Ernesto Morales were fluent in Spanish, and one was always at my elbow when I was interviewing or examining applicants.

XLII

Border Quarantine

Border Inspection

The Border Quarantine Inspectors represented four Agencies: Immigration, Customs, Agriculture, and Public Health. Almost all were retired military Chief Petty Officers (CPOs) with at least 20 years of experience.

There were usually four automobile lanes crossing into California, and each agency placed a Primary Screening inspector in a lane. Every Primary inspector was trained to screen for all four of the agencies. For example, each of my sixteen Public Health inspectors were also trained in issues relating to the other three agencies.

In addition to the man in Primary Screening (the auto lane), each Agency had two or more inspectors in the Secondary Inspection Area, to follow up on suspicious cases referred to them from the Primary Lane.

So if my Public Health inspector suspected an issue relating to agriculture, immigration, or customs, he would send the car over to the appropriate Secondary Inspection Area, where members of that Agency would evaluate or examine in depth. My border inspectors were all retired CPOs, most of whom had been Medical Corpsmen, so they were very familiar with health issues.

Other agents in Primary referred medical conditions to my inspectors in Secondary, and if my guys had any difficulty dealing with the case, they would call me out on the line to take a look and make a decision. We could send sick people back over the border or refer them for US medical care if they were otherwise qualified to enter the country. My team also performed those screening chest X-rays on 300 daily applicants under a *Bracero* (temporary agricultural worker) *Program*.

Seaport and Airport

Our Quarantine Station also had at least one inspector on duty at the airport doing the same (four part) screening, as well as insecticide-spraying the interiors of aircraft arriving from certain endemic infection countries. At the harbor they examined both passengers and cargo. Occasionally I'd be called out to either location to render a decision.

Christmas visit party from sister Sally at the O Club.

In one memorable case, my inspector refused the unloading of a shipload of some species of *Whitefish*, which was forbidden by the regulations at the time. My inspector refused a large bribe by the owner, who then called his US Congressman, who called Dr. Rosenblum, who then called me to confirm our actions, and to be sure that I congratulated my inspector. The fish were dumped.

Screening for Other Agencies

My inspectors taught me a lot about the regulations of the other border Agencies: *Agriculture* (prohibited certain plants, seeds, or plant diseases, as well as wild animals); *Customs* (prohibited certain imports--especially some artworks and loads of cash–meds and illegal drugs); and *Immigration* (falsified passports, illegal visas, counterfeit green cards, etc.)

Challenges

The usual challenges on the border were the smuggling of people and drugs, plants and animals. Secondary Inspectors would often find drugs packed in car door panels or spare tires, and people concealed in car trunks, and in barrels or crates in trucks. There was often excitement when a car's occupants–intercepted in Primary and referred to Secondary–would suddenly jump from their vehicle, abandon it, and race back across the border to avoid arrest. If the keys were gone, a tow truck was called to clear the lane. I was always impressed by how astute my guys were at detecting violations of all sorts.

Great Example

One event really impressed me with the expertise of my inspectors, and how really sharp they were.

One afternoon I was on the lane with Inspector Johnny Lawrence when a car returning from Mexico with California plates arrived. There was a big bouquet of flowers on the front seat. Lawrence asked him about his visit to Mexico. The guy replied that he had only gone to Tijuana to buy flowers for his mother's birthday party in San Diego. "They are much cheaper in Tijuana," the guy told us. Lawrence then very politely directed him to Customs Secondary Inspection Area. The guy loudly protested that he'd be late for her party, but Lawrence calmly insisted, so the guy drove into Secondary, then leaped from his car and raced back across the border!

Surprised, I asked Lawrence whatever prompted him to send the guy to Secondary for carrying flowers to his mother. Lawrence replied, "His license plate numbers are from Alameda County, that's Oakland. Why would he drive five hundred miles to save ten bucks on a bouquet of flowers?"

In Secondary inspection they found that all his car seat cushions were stuffed with hundreds of pounds of illegal drugs! Lawrence was not surprised. "This happens every day," he said. My guys always amazed me, and I came to hold them all in my deepest respect. I was so proud of them all

Lovely Mary Jo with the bouffant ("bee-hive") hair style of the mid-'60s.

XLIII

New Life

Socializing

Mary Jo and I were happy to take advantage of the commissary and liquor store on the Naval Base and we were even invited to events at the Admiral Kidd Officers Club.

We really enjoyed our apartment neighbors, who recommended various restaurants and attractions in Coronado and San Diego, along with special highlights such as Balboa Park and the San Diego Zoo. We enjoyed monthly Dinner Theater events in San Diego, and it seems there were several popular musicals at the time: Camelot, West Side Story, Most Happy Fella, Pajama Game, Funny Thing Happened on the Way to the Forum, and more; terrific Dinner Theater. My Chief Inspector, Francisco (Paco) Rodriguez occasionally took us to the *Tijuana Fronton* for the exciting *Jai Alai* games. I had never seen this fast-paced sport, and it made for some really fun evenings.

Boating

At the southern end of Coronado is the magnificent Hotel del Coronado, built in 1888, and said to have been the country's first electrified hotel, which was personally supervised by Thomas Edison. They have a marvelous boathouse and marina on the Bay.

I can't remember how we found her, but we purchased a 34-foot cabin cruiser with a 75 hp outboard motor. We named her *Caduceus* (name for the traditional medical symbol for healing.)

We took Sunday picnic cruises up and down the magnificent San Diego Bay, and our engine was even strong enough to pull a water skier. Every visiting family member or friend was taken for a boat ride on the Bay. The following year I took her out to sea for overnight camping at the offshore islands or up to Mission Bay Marina, cooking supper aboard with my little hibachi. Such fun!

From our first California Christmas card.

The elaborate architecture of the Hotel Marina where we kept our boat.

Career Concerns

At this point my career plan was still family practice, and I used to say, "I wanna be the world's best GP!" My morning Coast Guard clinics gave me plenty of challenges to my general practice medical skills. (For example, many wives asked me to speak to their husbands about foreplay, and I lacked training as a sex therapist.) Every night I reviewed the challenging cases I had seen that morning. Additionally, to keep current in all medical disciplines, I spent hours nightly reviewing subscriptions to Pediatric Journals, Surgical Journals, Orthopedic and Gynecology Journals, etc. I loved it all, though it sure was time consuming!

But no matter how much time I spent every evening, I felt I was not covering everything and was falling behind in new developments and treatments. I began to think that to know "*almost everything* about *almost everything*" was probably a 24 hour-daily challenge, and completely impractical. There were no general or family practice residencies at the time. I began to wonder whether knowing "*almost everything* about *not everything*" made more sense. This meant choosing a medical specialty.

So the *realities* of my challenging general practice Outpatient Clinic led me to consider some changes to my career dreams.

Reflections

Months passed quickly and we were having lots of fun while I was learning so much in both clinic and border station. At year's end, my Coast Guard Clinic was merged with the nearby Balboa Naval Hospital Outpatient Clinic, so my job was now full-time on the border. I missed the family practice–young men, their wives, and kids–but I feel the clinic job *fulfilled a purpose* in reorienting my career plans. And it was my romantic teenage request for the Coast Guard which brought me into this clinic to experience (and decline) family practice. *Providence once more!*

Having a full day to complete my border work now made life less stressful. Dr. Barr and I were sharing most of the workload, although it seemed he took a lot of leave. We took turns on the regular drive to our desert station of El Centro/Calexico, where we did medical inspections. I recall it being a long, hot drive in 110-120-degree desert heat with no air conditioning in my government car. Glad I wasn't stationed there!

Tijuana Friend

On some days, Ana Maldonado and I went to lunch in Tijuana with her friend Dr. Juan Fuentes Angulo. She said he was probably the only really honest doctor in Tijuana, and we became good friends.

Booze Importer

I could buy inexpensive *gallon* bottles of *Oso Negro* (Black Bear) gin and vodka and bring them back over the border with us (duty free) in our government car. My Coronado apartment friends were happy to enjoy these inexpensive *imported* spirits.

XLIV

Side Job

X-Ray Fraud

Occasionally, I found a suspicious lung lesion during our screening (3" x 3") mini-film X-rays, and the applicant was asked to return to Tijuana for a standard-size (14" x 17") film, for more careful study. Sometimes the applicant would return with a perfect chest X-ray with no hint of any tubercular inflammation or calcification. This was clearly fraudulent, so we'd send the guy back again, this time with a referral to Dr. Angulo for an honest X-ray, which indeed showed the seriousness of the communicable lung disease. With a diagnosis of active tuberculosis, the guy was counseled to seek prompt medical treatment, and was returned to Mexico. Angulo said that there were several doctors in Tijuana who would sell a normal-looking X-ray to anyone. (I worried about the risks of radiation exposure to that poor person with a normal chest, who was being repeatedly re-X-rayed by an unscrupulous doctor who then sold his X-ray film.)

Habla Usted Espanol?

The following spring semester Mary Jo and I registered for an adult evening Spanish class at Coronado High School. It was probably the best language semester I've ever experienced. The teacher was very imaginative and taught us songs, poems, and expressions, in addition to the usual basic vocabulary and grammar. This proved a valuable adjunct to my "border Spanish" at the office. One of my favorite little poems I remember pretty well after over 60 years:

Tres Amigos
Yo tengo tres amigos, muy vieles y muy buenos;
Son estos compañeros: un burro y dos perros.
Mi burro anda firme, mis perros ladran bien,
Todo el mundo canta, y yo canto tambien!

My orphans visiting US Naval Air Station.

Orphan's Adventure

There were always a number of young boys selling chewing gum to cars waiting in line in Tijuana to cross the border. "*Chicles, chicles!*" they'd cry. Occasionally inspectors would let them into the office and give them a cup of water or a little pocket change. I made friends with several and was surprised to learn that they were *all orphans*.

I wanted to do a little something nice for these poor kids, so I got permission from an Immigration Inspector to bring them across the border for a little adventure in California. My three invited pals showed up with six of their friends! I packed all nine into my government car, and brought them across the border (technically illegal).

First, on the ferry to visit the San Diego Zoo for a few amazing hours, where they were really excited. Then back on the ferry to the North Island Naval Air Station, where I showed them some of the big ships and aircraft of the U.S. Navy.

Piñata Party

Finally, we drove to our apartment for a barbecue and piñata party in our back parking area. I had hung a large piñata filled with candies, small change, and trinkets. Neighbor Lt. Bob Otis and Mary Jo barbecued hamburgers, served punch, and provided cookies for dessert.

After having their fill, the boys took turns being blindfolded and swatting at the piñata with a stick in the usual way.

Finally, one of them ruptured the piñata, the goodies scattered all over, and the boys scrambled to grab their share. It was a lovely party, all great fun in the name of interna-

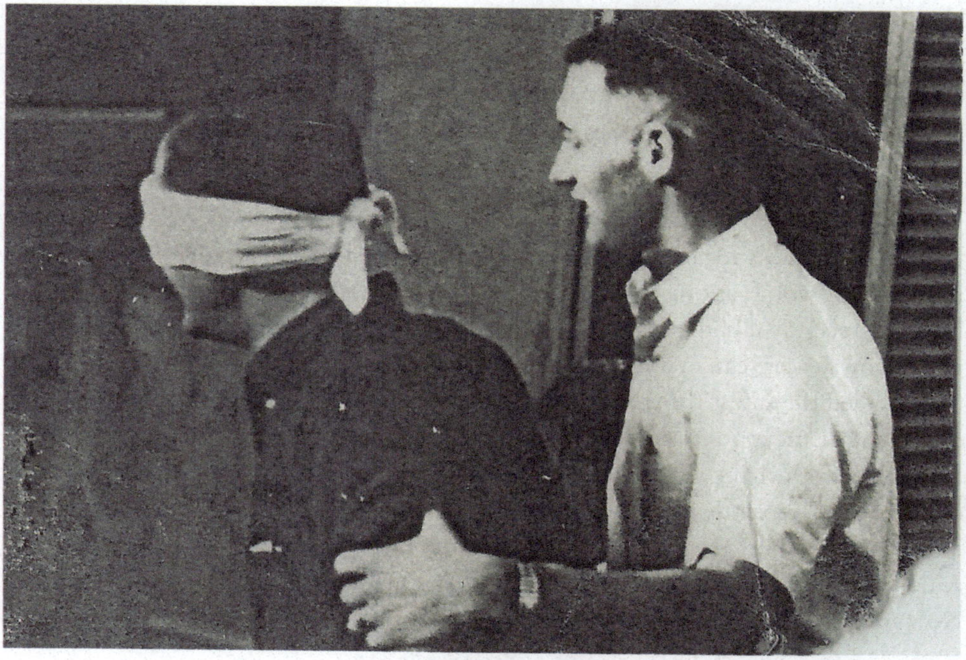

Bob Otis with blindfolded kids swatting the piñata!

tional hospitality and love, and after our drive to the border, they each happily returned to Tijuana carrying their bags of loot.

Side Job

By this time my brother Bob had finished college, served his two years with the Army artillery in Viet Nam, and became an Underwriter with New York Life Insurance Company (NYLIC) in Honolulu. I'm not sure how it happened, but shortly thereafter I was contacted by a San Diego NYLIC agent and asked if I would be willing to do insurance physicals in the homes of clients unable or unwilling to visit a doctor's office. I soon was spending an evening a week driving into the suburbs with my blood pressure cuff, bathroom scale, stethoscope, urine cans, and medical exam forms, doing brief screening exams on clients in their homes.

My favorite firearm, S&W .38 cal Police Special.

It was a pleasant side job. I grew familiar with the suburbs, and I think I earned $20 apiece. The word spread and I was soon serving half a dozen agents which kept me pretty busy several nights a week.

One of my inspectors asked if I felt uncomfortable alone at night in some uncertain neighborhoods.

I had not felt in any danger, but he suggested I might want to consider carrying a handgun. I thought that it couldn't hurt, and the previous Christmas Mary Jo had given me my favorite gun of all time, a .38 caliber S&W 4" Police Special revolver, just like the six-shooter cowboy guns in the movies that had thrilled us in grade school.

Concealed Carry

California's laws regarding carrying guns were considered ambiguous at best, contradictory at worst: at one time, a gun must be *concealed* in the car trunk or the glove box. But recently it had been declared that the gun must be *displayed*: visible on one's person, on the car seat, or atop the dashboard.

I decided the safest thing would be to get a concealed-carry permit. So I applied, and soon had an appointment to bring my gun to a meeting with a San Diego Sheriff. I explained my driving alone at night. He reviewed gun safety and reminded me of the danger of inadvertently injuring myself or another with my firearm.

He examined my revolver, and after assuring that it was empty, he handed it back and said, "Okay, now pretend I'm a mugger and you want to pull your gun on me, OK? Now go ahead!" I pulled out my gun and pointed at him.

Gun Grab!

Lightning fast, he karate-chopped my wrist, which caused my hand to spring open, losing my grip. With his other hand, he caught the tumbling pistol, spun it around with both hands, and now pointed it at me! This all happened within a second! I was stunned to realize how quickly he had disarmed me! And then with a smirk, he said, "And now, how does it feel to be shot by your own gun? You'd have been *safer with no gun!*" I got the message!

He then pointed out that when I pulled my gun on him, I should have stepped back several feet, so that I would be out of reach of his lightning karate-chop. It was an excellent lesson I've never forgotten.

Soon I received my *License to Carry Concealed Pistol, Revolver, or Other Firearm.* I carried the weapon with me in the car and never needed to even consider reaching for it. The following month, I got a permit to carry on the Naval Base, for the convenience of keeping it in the car on base. Better to have a gun and not need it than to need a gun and not have it.

A Border Patrol buddy even gave me his used holster and gun cartridge belt, which I've always treasured.

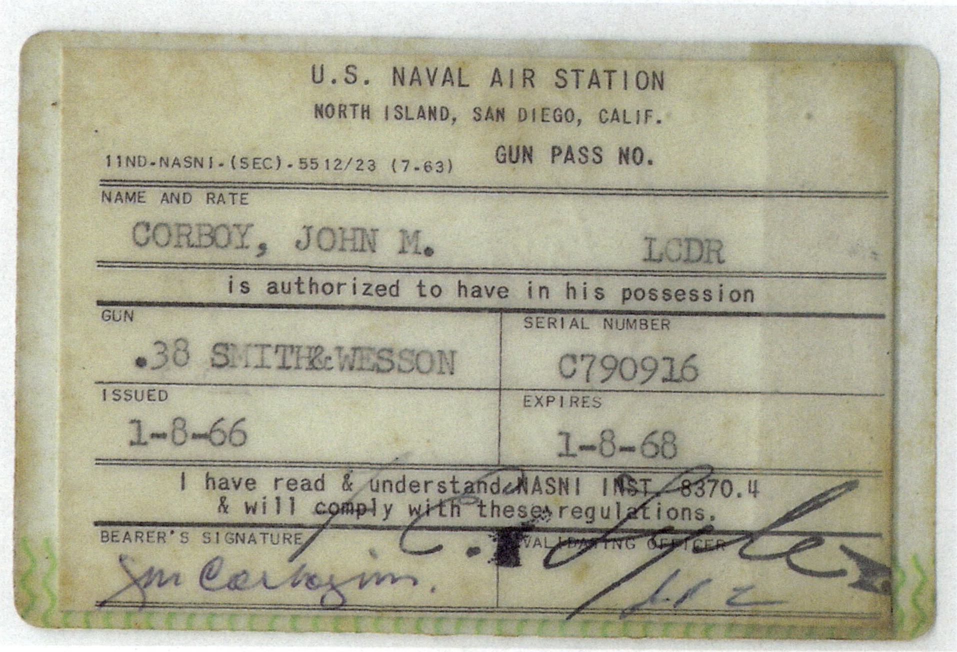

U.S. NAVAL AIR STATION
NORTH ISLAND, SAN DIEGO, CALIF.

11ND-NASNI-(SEC)-5512/23 (7-63) GUN PASS NO.

NAME AND RATE
CORBOY, JOHN M. LCDR

is authorized to have in his possession

GUN	SERIAL NUMBER
.38 SMITH&WESSON	C790916
ISSUED	EXPIRES
1-8-66	1-8-68

I have read & understand NASNI INST 8370.4
& will comply with these regulations.

BEARER'S SIGNATURE VALIDATING OFFICER

Naval Base Gun Pass.

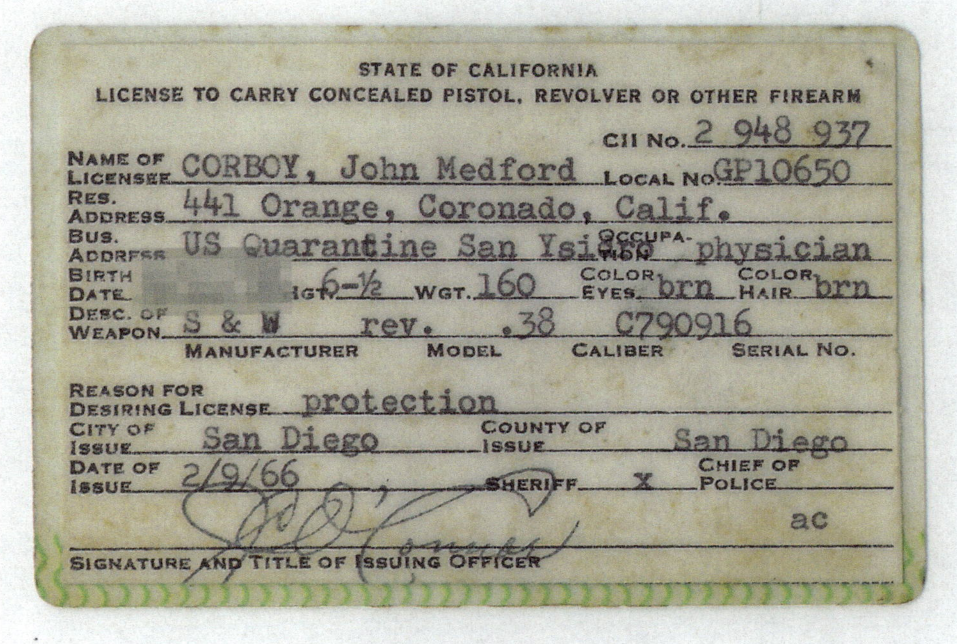

STATE OF CALIFORNIA
LICENSE TO CARRY CONCEALED PISTOL, REVOLVER OR OTHER FIREARM

CII No. 2 948 937

NAME OF LICENSEE CORBOY, John Medford LOCAL NO. GP10650
RES. ADDRESS 441 Orange, Coronado, Calif.
BUS. ADDRESS US Quarantine San Ysidro OCCUPATION physician
BIRTH DATE [redacted] 6-½ WGT. 160 COLOR EYES brn COLOR HAIR brn
DESC. OF WEAPON S & W rev. .38 C790916
MANUFACTURER MODEL CALIBER SERIAL NO.

REASON FOR DESIRING LICENSE protection
CITY OF ISSUE San Diego COUNTY OF ISSUE San Diego
DATE OF ISSUE 2/9/66 SHERIFF X CHIEF OF POLICE

ac

SIGNATURE AND TITLE OF ISSUING OFFICER

My California license to carry a concealed firearm.

XLV

LIESURE HOURS

Yosemite Reunion

In the spring of '65 we took our first trip to Yosemite National Park to camp with my best man, Dave Roseman and his wife Joan, MJ's Matron of Honor. He had not yet been drafted, so he entered his Surgical Residency, and with his modest new salary, had purchased a magnificent new '64 Chevrolet Corvette *Stingray* convertible. They had enjoyed their cross-country drive from Chicago in this powerful, classy sports car. We delighted in several days of camping, hiking, horseback riding, and sharing stories of our latest career moves.

Returning home from Yosemite we stopped in San Francisco to enjoy Fisherman's Wharf, then drove down the coast to San Simeon, where we loved touring the Hearst Castle. Reaching Los Angeles, we enjoyed our first visit to Disneyland, where admission was still $7.80 and Knott's Berry Farm, where admission was still free!

Cioppino Chef

In San Diego near the Coronado ferry wharf was a fabulous fish market. Mary Jo would often visit there, befriending the mongers, who gave her valuable advice for cooking fish, crabs, and clams. I had come across an outstanding recipe for *Cioppino*, an Italian tomato-red wine-based seafood stew, and we could collect all the ingredients at this fish market. Every few weeks I prepared my Cioppino for visitors and neighbors. The recipe served six or more, so we became frequent dinner hosts. Mary Jo made some large, much appreciated, bibs for the diners, since cracking lobsters, opening clams and mussels, and spearing shrimp and fish, all smothered in tomato sauce, was always deliciously messy.

Visiting Friends

We enjoyed visits from my high school pal, Don Doyle, as well as my med school cadaver-beer-motorcycle buddy, Dave Cope, who was in his Pediatrics Residency.

High school buddy Don Doyle and wife Vanita.

Med school bike buddy Dave Cope and me, with our matching hillbilly hats and engraved mugs.

Dave brought us matching hillbilly hats, and I shared matching engraved beer mugs. MJ and I had great fun boating and partying with all our visitors.

Deputy Arrives

Dr. Barr left in June, and I became the boss MOC. My Deputy, Dr. Mike Geyser, fresh from his orientation in El Paso, arrived the first week in July, '65. I helped with his border orientation and training, and Mary Jo and I very much enjoyed socializing with Mike and his wife Joyce.

So thoughtful! I've always treasured this certificate as much as those I actually earned!

Promotion!

When I took over as Medical Officer in Charge, I was pleasantly surprised to receive a promotion: I was now ranked a PHS Senior Assistant Surgeon: SAS (M) (R) (T) (Meaning Medical, Reserve, Temporary). This was the equivalent of a Naval Lieutenant Commander (O4), with a raise in pay and a new set of collar devices and distinctive shoulder boards for my uniform.

Mayor!

Naval officers are typically quite rank-conscious, and when he learned of my promotion to Lt. Commander, our landlord, retired Naval Captain Ray Madsen, who earlier had "The Village" inscribed on the street front of our building, presented me with a certificate proclaiming me as *Mayor of the Village*, I suppose because I was the highest-ranking officer in his building. Who, me?

Biking Again

That spring my motorcycle dealer pal in Chicago, Dudley Brattin, who had relocated his BMW dealership to San Diego, came to Coronado with a couple of familiar BMWs. We rode together, touring the nearby countryside. It was fun to be riding in uniform on the Naval Base.

I loved riding on the Naval Base in uniform.

XLVI

New Career Plan

Career Change

By summer I had decided that *mastering* General Practice was too much for me, and I should choose a medical specialty. The one I knew the most about was *ophthalmology* (medical, optical, and surgical eye care), my father's profession. In elementary school I had attended some of his volunteer classes for the student nurses at Queens and St. Francis Hospitals in Honolulu, and I was fascinated by the large eye models that he used for training.

Dad had also invited me to his operating room to watch some eye surgery when I was in high school. Ophthalmology seemed to be very gratifying: people's vision could be restored, crossed eyes straightened, cataracts removed, lids repaired, retinas re-attached, glasses and contact lenses prescribed, etc. Also, there were the advantages that patients seldom called after midnight, and rarely died.

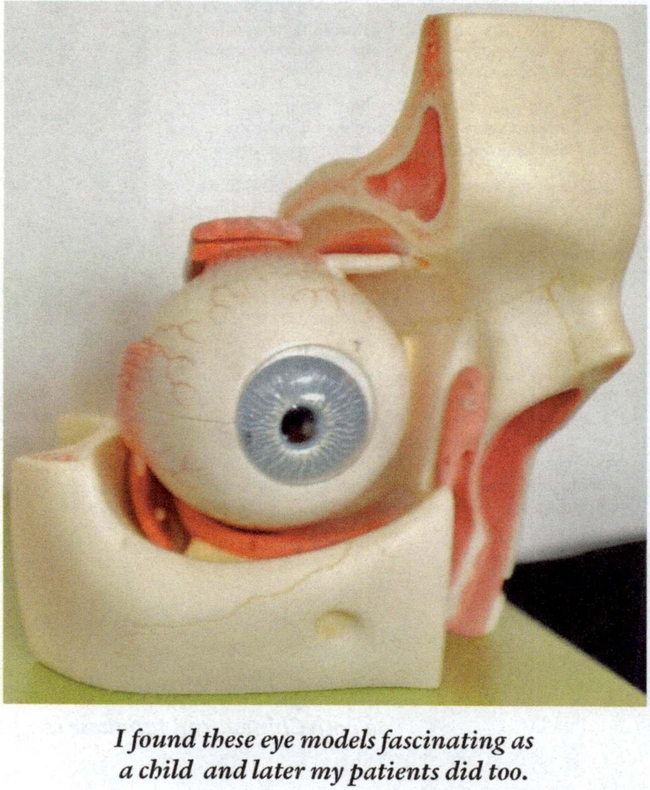

I found these eye models fascinating as a child and later my patients did too.

My dad was very happy with his practice, doing

A Chinese Japanese Projectochart Slide

PHILIP M. CORBOY, M.D., HONOLULU

WHEN MY JAPANESE PROJECTOCHART slide was introduced in August of 1956,[1] it was evident in the practice of ophthalmology in Honolulu and other similarly populated centers, which are multilingual, and in which a large segment of the population are of oriental extraction, that to properly test vision with Japanese who were not familiar with English characters currently employed (Snellen), it was necessary to provide a test slide using Japanese characters. That Projectochart slide, per se, functioned to great advantage.

Subsequently, it has been found that among other oriental races, the Chinese and Koreans particularly, that a Projectochart slide using their characters also was highly desirable. This need has given place to the design and production of a new Projectochart slide[2] which has been divided into two halves, one Chinese characters, which also can be used by Koreans, the other half Japanese characters, which are easily understood by both Japanese and Okinawans.

The requirements of Snellen type, i.e., that the characters subtend an angle of 5 minutes of arc, have been adhered to with great accuracy.

Characters varying from 20/300 to 20/15 are now available in stepdown sizes. There are quite a number of characters that are common to both Chinese and Japanese, and this fact was taken advantage of by using only one such common character for the 20/300 line, two such for the 20/200 line, and four for the 20/100 line on the projectochart slide.

The 20/80 line in this new slide is unique in that it contains a built-in bichromatic testing facility. The left half of the line is red, the right half green, on which have been superimposed four equal circles or Landolt's rings, which fit evenly into the projected square of the image on the screen, and which do not necessitate the addition of a colored filter being drawn over them. This facilitates quick use of the bichromatic testing function, with disregard to either oriental characters, and without loss of time by the examiner.

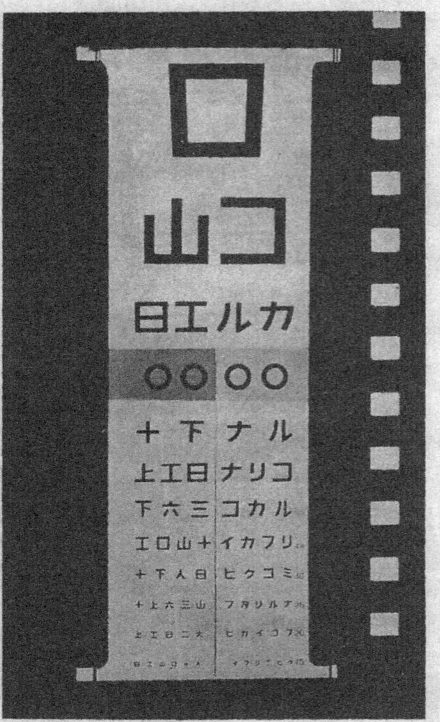

Below the 20/80 line, are eight lines of evenly numbered and divided characters. Chinese and Japanese, ranging from 20/70 to 20/15 inclusive.

JUNE, 1960 29

This unique eye chart consists of characters common to both Chinese and Japanese languages.

a lot of free care for the indigent, and taking regular trips to the neighboring islands with the Lions Clubs for volunteer screening clinics. He had even designed a Chinese-Japanese Eye Chart for his elderly Asian patients.

Although he had never encouraged me toward medicine, much less ophthalmology, I knew both of us would appreciate my emulating him and his wonderful humanitarian example.

Residency

I learned that the Public Health Service had an Ophthalmology Residency Program in four locations, one of which was in San Francisco. I composed letters of inquiry, followed by forms of application. As a PHS Commissioned Officer (O-4), I knew my pay would be higher than in a standard hospital residency training program. But the PHS residency attraction was to remain in uniform, which I was enjoying.

CGAS Flight

Through the kindness of some of my former Coast Guard patients, I hopped a helicopter training flight to Los Angeles.

From LA I flew commercial air up to San Francisco for an interview with the Chief of the Eye Department and Residency Program, Dr. William (Bill) Richards. The training was held in the large USPHS Hospital at 14th Avenue and Lake Street, in view of the

All suited up as a Coast Guard medic for my flight.

Golden Gate Bridge. Pretty exciting!

Dr. Richards told me that there had been a question of sufficient academic training in his program, despite its affiliation with the Ophthalmology Residency Program, University of California, San Francisco. This situation might affect future Accreditation of his PHS Residency Program. So he had arranged for his first-year resident to be enrolled in the ophthalmology residency training at Washington University – Barnes/McMillan Eye Hospital in St. Louis. This was even more exciting, because I had learned this was a renowned academic training program led by the esteemed Prof. Bernard Becker, MD. What a terrific opportunity: a first-year trainee in this envied program!

Subsequently, I made a great effort to impress Dr. Richards with my desirability as his next first-year resident. I had a number of letters of recommendation sent to him and assured him that I would be proud to represent his program in St. Louis. I'd do my best to impress Dr. Becker with my hard work and PHS enthusiasm, hoping Richards could send future San Francisco PHS first-year residents to St. Louis.

Acceptance!

These efforts seemed successful, because that fall I received notice of my acceptance in the USPHS San Francisco Ophthalmology Residency '66 -'69 Program! I promptly thanked Dr. Richards for his support and sent letters of appreciation to those who had submitted recommendations on my behalf.

Payback

With my acceptance came the reminder that for each year of PHS Residency Training, I was expected to serve a year as a specialist in a PHS Hospital or training program, a so-called "pay-back". This would mean a six-year commitment. I was considering a possible career as a USPHS Commissioned Officer, so this did not seem a difficult request.

I began receiving orientation materials from St. Louis, and among these was a letter from a Dr. George Bresnick, a senior resident in Dr.Becker's program. Bresnick wrote that after his residency graduation, he was doing a year of postgraduate eye research in London. He offered me his furnished apartment for my year in St. Louis if I'd pay the rent. Then he'd take it back on his return, when he planned to join Dr. Becker's faculty. Well, this could not be better news: I now had a furnished apartment, convenient to the training hospital, awaiting me in St. Louis! *Providence?*

Travel Fun

We did a lot of travel during my second border year, now that I had an assistant to cover for me. Mary Jo and I flew an Aeronaves de Mexico five-city tour of Mexico, took a drive to Los Angeles, another to Las Vegas, even a trip to the Grand Canyon. We often camped in the nearby mountains and rented a Navy Exchange camping trailer for a couple of these weekend trips.

Rose Parade

On New Year's Day '65 and '66, we joined our apartment pals on a charter bus from the Navy Exchange up to see the Rose Parade in Pasadena. We all celebrated our *New Year's Eve party* early in one of the apartments, set the clock three hours ahead, partied until "midnight" (9 PM), and crashed into bed until 2 AM, to meet the 3 AM bus. Our tickets gave us great bleacher seats, and we savored the spectacle.

Dinner Fun

We took a car trip to La Paz, Mexico with one of my favorite inspectors, Johnny Lawrence and his wife. Along the way we enjoyed a delicious fish in a little restaurant, and Johnny, in his best border-Spanish, asked what kind of fish it was. The waiter replied, "*Pescado*."

Well, that's the Spanish word for *fish*. So Johnny persisted, trying to learn the *name* of this *Pescado*. The conversation went back and forth, and was so funny, but we never did learn the name, other than it was "*Pescado-fish*."

Another equally amusing dinner moment occurred while Mary Jo and I were dining in a lovely San Diego restaurant and I inquired of the waitress,

"What is the *soup du jour*?"

She replied, rather haughtily,

"That's the soup of the day!"

I thanked her, "But *what is* the soup of the day?"

"I told you," she said impatiently,

"It's French, called the '*soup du jour*'!"

Not one to quit, I finally said,

"Okay, please tell me *what flavor* is the *soup du jour*?"

"Oh", she replied, seeming relieved, "It's pea soup."

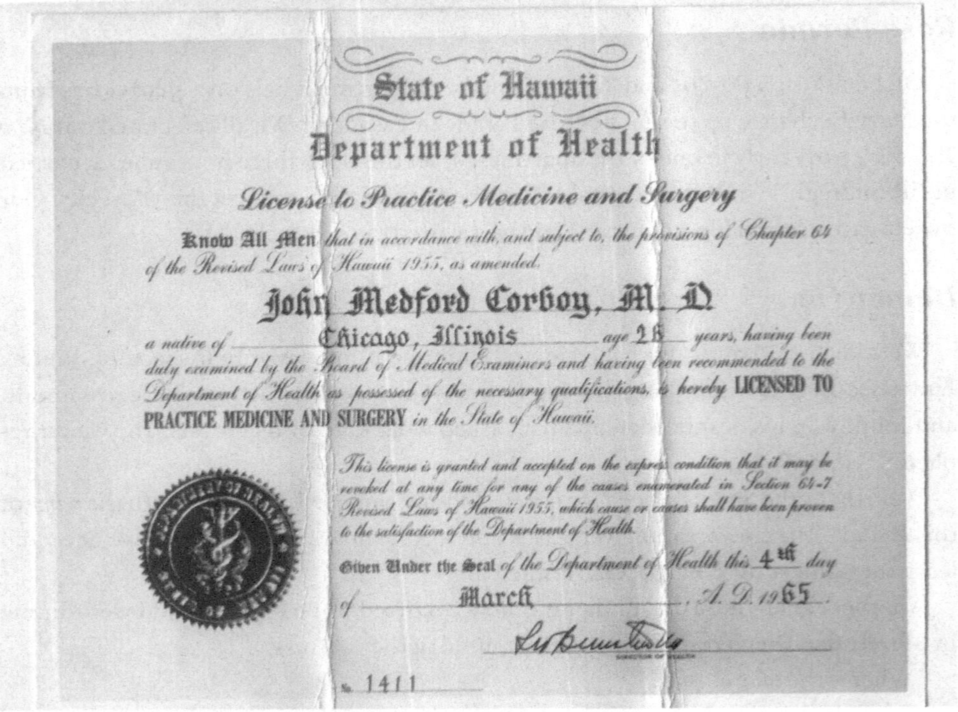

State of Hawaii

Department of Health

License to Practice Medicine and Surgery

Know All Men that in accordance with, and subject to, the provisions of Chapter 64 of the Revised Laws of Hawaii 1955, as amended,

John Medford Corboy, M. D.

a native of Chicago, Illinois age 28 years, having been duly examined by the Board of Medical Examiners and having been recommended to the Department of Health as possessed of the necessary qualifications, is hereby LICENSED TO PRACTICE MEDICINE AND SURGERY in the State of Hawaii.

This license is granted and accepted on the express condition that it may be revoked at any time for any of the causes enumerated in Section 64-7 Revised Laws of Hawaii 1955, which cause or causes shall have been proven to the satisfaction of the Department of Health.

Given Under the Seal of the Department of Health this 4th day of March, A. D. 1965.

Director of Health

No. 1411

I passed the exam for Hawaii licensure.

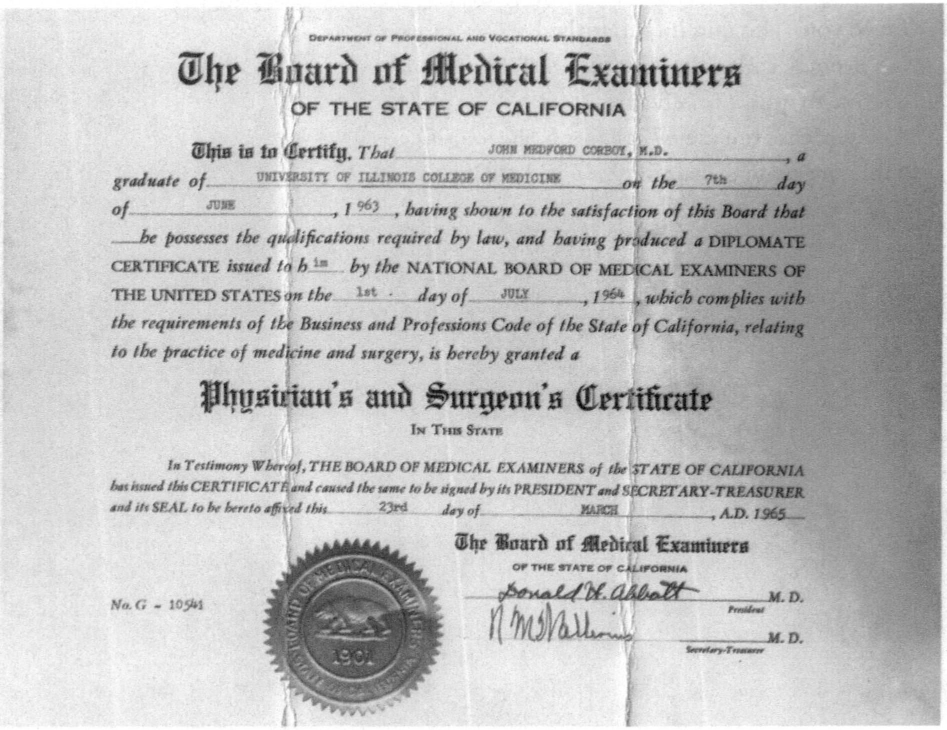

Department of Professional and Vocational Standards

The Board of Medical Examiners

OF THE STATE OF CALIFORNIA

This is to Certify, That JOHN MEDFORD CORBOY, M.D., a graduate of UNIVERSITY OF ILLINOIS COLLEGE OF MEDICINE on the 7th day of JUNE, 1963, having shown to the satisfaction of this Board that he possesses the qualifications required by law, and having produced a DIPLOMATE CERTIFICATE issued to him by the NATIONAL BOARD OF MEDICAL EXAMINERS OF THE UNITED STATES on the 1st day of JULY, 1964, which complies with the requirements of the Business and Professions Code of the State of California, relating to the practice of medicine and surgery, is hereby granted a

Physician's and Surgeon's Certificate

In This State

In Testimony Whereof, THE BOARD OF MEDICAL EXAMINERS of the STATE OF CALIFORNIA has issued this CERTIFICATE and caused the same to be signed by its PRESIDENT and SECRETARY-TREASURER and its SEAL to be hereto affixed this 23rd day of MARCH, A.D. 1965

The Board of Medical Examiners

OF THE STATE OF CALIFORNIA

No. G - 10541

Donald H. Abbott M. D.
President

M. D.
Secretary-Treasurer

Glad to pass exam for California licensure, as well.

XLVII

SAD FAREWELL

Licensure

Earlier, I had flown home to take my State Medical Board exam for Hawaii licensure, before I forgot too much from my internship studies. This was like most general medical examinations, except there was a special section on *leprosy* and we were shown several patients with the clinical signs of leprosy or *Hansen's Disease*, which had been prevalent in Hawaii in the previous century among Polynesians, who were especially susceptible due to their lack of immunity. There were still leprosy patients to be seen, in addition to those quarantined on Molokai.

Once I knew I would be doing my residency in San Francisco, this year I took the Medical Board Examinations for California licensure, and passed those, as well.

We loved our Volvo wagon, drove it for almost a decade.

New Car

Since we'd be driving to St. Louis with more possessions than we had when traveling to California two years ago in the *Spitfire*, we decided we had outgrown the little sports car and it was time for something larger. We chose a '66 Volvo Station Wagon.

This had all the benefits of an American wagon but was more compact. Since we'd be driving in the summer, we had air-conditioning installed.

HISTORICAL NOTE

In 1966, cars with air-conditioning, so-called "factory air", were a rarity, and local distributors did the after-market installations.

Departure

Meanwhile, part of our departure planning was to sell our beloved *Caduceus*. We had her hauled out, cleaned up, painted, bottom scraped and treated with anti-fouling copper sulfate paint, and engine tuned. She was really a beauty, but she unaccountably remained on the market week after week. We became quite concerned as our departure date approached and were deeply relieved when she finally sold. For a sailor it is said, "His *second-happiest* day is the day he buys his boat. His *happiest* day is when he's able to sell his boat!"

Portrait for boat sale.

Receiving the mug from Chief Inspector Purlia and senior staff.

Great sentimental treasure, signed by all my fabulous staff!

Adios!

The month before departure was a busy one. Dr. Angulo gave me a gift of a new suit, tailored for me in Tijuana. Dr. Geyser took over my job as MOC and awaited his incoming deputy.

My quarantine staff hosted a wonderful departure party for Mary Jo and me at their CPO Club, and---as a tribute to my caffeine habits---gave me a beautiful coffee mug decorated with all their signatures.

Our Orange Avenue neighbors gave us a rousing send-off at the Naval Admiral Kidd Officers Club. Leaving these very special military pals, mostly fighter pilots, was especially painful.

Mary Jo sold her car, we loaded up the Volvo wagon, bid sad final farewells, and crossed the Bay on our final ferry ride, heading for St. Louis. What amazing learning experiences and adventures we'd had in just two years! On the way we'd see my sister and husband in Denver, as well as Mary Jo's family and our medical friends and Phil Miller in Chicago, before heading to St. Louis, all the while very grateful for our new auto air-conditioning!

Family Planning

On the way we discussed starting a family. We had sensibly agreed on a two-year marriage trial, to see how well we got along with each other, before adding additional family members. Those two years were happily successful, because we were both flexible, respectful, and supportive of each other. We felt confident that we could cooperate and manage the stresses of child-rearing. We had a bigger car now, and both wanted kids, so maybe St. Louis would be the place to start our family. As we headed toward 9115 Wrenwood Lane, Brentwood, Missouri, a St. Louis suburb, we realized that we'd have a new home, I'd begin training for a new ophthalmic career, and plan for a new family member. Lots of *new stuff* ahead! Heading into the land of Mark Twain, BBQ, and Budweiser, sounded like fun!

Look for Volume 3: "Eyes and Cries" Residency and New Family

COMING SOON!

"On to St. Louis! Beginning a specialty career! Starting a family! Wow, pretty exciting adventures ahead! What will come of this next challenging step?"

This is the story of my residency training in ophthalmology (eye diseases and surgery) in St. Louis and San Francisco. Then my first job as a fledgling ophthalmologist, along with our joy in raising our three marvelous children.

I hope you'll enjoy **Volume Three**, "Eyes and Cries" of Life and Times of "Little Johnny Corboy"

About the Author

JOHN M. CORBOY grew up in Hawai'i, attending first Punahou then St. Louis School. He completed his pre-medical training at Loyola University in Chicago and earned his MD from the University of Illinois, Chicago. After completing his internship at Rush-Presbyterian Hospital, he served in the USPHS as medical officer for the US Coast Guard Air Station Clinic in San Diego and for two years as Medical Officer in Charge (MOC) of San Ysidro Border Quarantine Station.

He served his Ophthalmology residency with Washington University/ Barnes McMillan Hospital in St. Louis and the USPHS Hospital in San Francisco.

Returning to Hawai'i he practiced Ophthalmology with Kaiser Permanente Medical Group, and in 1975 he opened his Hawaiian Eye Center as Surgeon-Director, which grew to a statewide network of nine offices. In 1979 Corboy created the annual Hawaiian Eye Meeting, which still serves the profession today after forty-four years. On his retirement after thirty years in ophthalmic practice, he gave a further twenty-two years to hundreds of charity medical missions worldwide and Asian training programs through his Hawaiian Eye Foundation.

After his second retirement, from the foundation, he has returned to his interest in writing by describing all the fun and joy he has experienced in life in the five-volume series *The Life and Times of "Little Johnny Corboy"*, the first volume of which is presented here: *Providence in the Pacific*.

Beloved dearest college buddy and long time friend.

Rest in peace.

Allen Edward Zencka M.D.
January 26, 1939–April 14, 2021

Made in the USA

Made in the USA
Columbia, SC
25 September 2024

42918937R00124